W9-CDI-806

BUILDING LEADERSHIP BRIDGES 2001

Shelly Wilsey,
Larraine R. Matusak and
Cynthia Cherrey, Editors

International Leadership Association
The James MacGregor Burns
Academy of Leadership

Table of Contents

INTRODUCTION

WITH EACH NEW YEAR, THE INTERNATIONAL LEADERSHIP ASSOCIATION (ILA) grows and evolves, displaying creative and exciting new ideas. *Building Leadership Bridges, 2001* is evidence of ILA's growth and maturity, and it is our hope that it will make a powerful impact on leadership theory and practice worldwide.

This monograph reflects the finest work of scholars and practitioners who participated in the ILA conference held in Toronto, Canada, in November 2000. In it, you'll find the keynote addresses and several other papers that were of particular interest to both scholars and practitioners. We sought to create a mix—a meeting of the minds between those who study leadership and those who practice it.

It is our intent that this publication receive wide distribution among individuals and organizations with a professional interest in leadership. It can be used as a resource in leadership development programs and classrooms. We hope you will use it as a tool to encourage others to join the ILA.

We especially want to thank ILA Program Director Shelly Wilsey for her hard work as lead editor. We also want to thank Stefanie Weiss and Barbara Shapiro for their assistance.

The International Leadership Association, a testament to the fact that leadership matters, was born just a few years ago. In that short period of time, ILA has come to represent a burgeoning global network for all those with a professional interest in leadership. Its mission is to meet annually to:

- generate and disseminate cutting-edge work in theory and practice;
- strengthen ties among those who study, teach and exercise leadership; and
- serve as an arena within which those with a professional interest in leadership can share research, resources, information and ideas.

It is the vision of ILA's founders and board members that, within the next decade, ILA will be recognized around the world as the preeminent forum for cutting-edge thinking in leadership scholarship and practice. *Building Leadership Bridges, 2001* is one step along the way to make that happen.

CYNTHIA CHERREY
Executive Director, ILA

LARRAINE R. MATUSAK
Chair, ILA Program Committee; Senior Scholar, Academy of Leadership

Note: Not all of the excellent presentations at ILA's 2000 conference could be included in this book. You can find more on ILA's Web site at www.academy.umd.edu/ila.

Women and Leadership: Looking Back, Looking Forward

By The Right Honorable Kim Campbell

ONE OF THE ANOMALIES OF THE 20TH CENTURY IS HOW LITTLE the political gains won in the early years of the century have been reflected at the top of the political process.

Women first got the vote in 1893 in New Zealand. In Canada women got the vote in 1917. In 1920, the United States was the twenty-first country to give women the vote. Many European countries did not give women the vote until after World War II. In Latin America, Ecuador was the first in 1929. Mexico did not allow women to vote until 1953. In Asia, it might interest you to know, Mongolia was the first country to give women the vote in 1923. Japan and South Korea did not give women the vote until after the war in 1945. In Africa, women won the right to vote beginning in the 1940s and continuing until the 1970s. Generally, African women were enfranchised as former colonies achieved independence.

When we look back even a few decades, it always seemed disheartening to think about the chances of girls getting elected even to student council president in high school. Now it seems like old history; surely we have moved so much further.

But a recent parliamentary study of 65 countries shows that only 15 percent of the lawmakers in those countries are women. Fifteen percent! In Canada fewer than one-third of the members of Parliament are women. There was only one woman prime minister and just two women provincial premiers, and, incidentally, only one of those three women, Catherine Callbeck, premier of Prince Edward Island, was actually elected in the general election.

In the United States, 20 percent of elected officials nationwide are women. Prior to the 2000 elections, there were only nine female senators and three female governors. Prior to the 2000 elections, women held only 15.3 percent of the seats in the U.S. House of Representatives. The United States ranks forty-second in the world in terms of representation of women. Sweden ranks number one, as 45 percent of its national legislators are women.

But dreary as those figures are, between 1975 and 1995 female legislators in Western countries doubled their percentage of representation. While this is twice as good as it was in 1975, the question is really, Why so few?

Despite the fact that women have had the vote for several generations now, why are we still only 15 percent of the lawmakers in democracies? Why indeed, when women have always led when they had the chance.

Historical Role Models

I found some great examples of powerful women in Jacques Barzun's new book, *From Dawn to Decadence.* In this wonderful story, Barzun identifies a number of women in the 16th century who were powerful in Europe. You will recall Elizabeth I, of course, a woman I have read about and admired my whole life. He also makes interesting reference to powerful women politicians in the Vatican. Evidently the sisters and the female relatives of the popes and cardinals played a very significant role in what must have been remarkably complex politics in that center of power.

Even in the 16th century some brave men championed the notion of women's equality, but they were quickly dismissed because, after all, the scriptures specified women's weakness and one could not claim any qualities that went against scriptural authority.

Women got their chance to lead through birth and through dynastic connections, or occasionally by marriage, as in the case of Catherine the Great. The reign of Elizabeth I is a perfect example of the axiom that blood is thicker than water. It seems that people would rather have had the daughter of King Henry the VIII than someone outside the family. As the reasoning goes, if Henry can't provide us with a son, well, at least we will have a touch of the old king in his daughter and that is better than looking someplace else. In other words, people believed that dynasty will help create some kind of stability in an uncertain world.

Not so in today's world. Let me turn to a recent U.S. survey in which 90 percent of those responding said that they would vote for a woman president if she were qualified. That's some Catch 22 — "if she were qualified." Women were rated higher than men on the factors of trustworthiness and honesty and on the ability to understand ordinary people. And yet there seems to be a perception that a male president is more effective, especially in the ability to lead a nation in a crisis and the ability to make difficult decisions.

Looking back at the women who had the chance to lead through history, this distinction does not seem to be borne out. Can Elizabeth I be described as somebody who could not lead a nation through a crisis or who could not make difficult decisions? Hardly. Instead, Elizabeth I is seen as an exception to the rule or an anomaly or really overrated and not, in fact, as good as people say.

Paul Johnson wrote a wonderful book on this topic called *Elizabeth I: A Study of Power and Intellect,* in which he looks at the attempts by historians to downgrade Elizabeth's accomplishments. This is a woman whom Jacques Barzun describes as "one of the most learned people of her age." She wrote poetry in Greek and she had an extraordinary mind, but if you accept the fact that she was really good, then maybe there is more to her. Frightening prospect! Historians have explained the fact away by saying that people fawned over her because she was the Queen and she wasn't really very clever. If she were living next door to you, they say, you wouldn't be impressed.

Countering the Stereotypes

A number of current studies show that when people are asked to identify the qualities of masculinity and the qualities of femininity and the qualities of leadership, there is a great correlation between the qualities attributed to masculinity and those attributed to leadership.

How can we handle these stereotypes? I suggest three approaches. First is what I call gender literacy. For a long time, women worried about studies that identified differences in gender. It always seemed that if there were differences between men and women, those differences would be used to justify the exclusion of women, particularly those who were trying to focus on the notion that men and women were the same.

What in fact has turned out to be the case is that studies that look at differences between men and women do not justify the exclusion of woman at all. In many cases they find attributes in women that make them extremely desirable candidates for careers that they have not traditionally been welcome to enter.

Judy Rosener, a professor at the University of California at Irvine's Graduate School of Management, published an article in *Harvard Business Review* in 1990 called "Ways Women Lead," and she followed that up with a book called *America's Competitive Secret: Women Managers.* Rosener interviewed women and men in 80 major corporations in the United States, looking at their leadership styles. She discovered that, in general, women tend to favor what she called the "interactive" style of leadership. This tends to be non-hierarchical, power-sharing, a rather looser style of leadership than that favored by men. Men tend to favor the "command and control " style of leadership, a more hierarchical style.

It is important to recognize that one is not better than the other. Each of these styles of leadership is in fact the optimal style for certain circumstances. If you are in the middle of a war, it's no time for everybody to sit around trying to come to consensus about where to go next. This situation cries out for a command-and-control style of leadership.

Rosener does not make this gender specific. She is a friend of the Clintons and thinks that Bill Clinton is an interactive leader and that Hillary Clinton is a command-and-control leader. So she makes the point that it is not a hard and fast rule about men and women, but that generally women tend to favor the interactive leadership style.

> **BUT THE BIG CATCH 22 IS THAT WHEN MEN USE AN INTERACTIVE MANAGEMENT MODE … THIS IS SEEN AS HIGHLY ADMIRABLE. BUT WHEN WOMEN DO IT, IT IS SOMETHING ATTRIBUTED TO GENDER AND NOT VALUED! YOU CAN'T WIN.**

What she found was that now, in this time of corporate flattening, particularly with the development of knowledge-based industries, the interactive style of leadership has become more appropriate. For example, if you are in Silicon Valley, and you have got a knowledge-based company, there is no "guy in the big corner office" who has a monopoly on information and "dispenses" wisdom down the hierarchy.

In fact, sometimes the most important person in the high-tech business is that obnoxious 20-year-old you just hired last week who has a bizarre haircut and an earring in his…whatever. This is no time to be hierarchical. So, as Judy Rosener describes it, men are now willing to be interactive leaders, because this is the style that is appropriate.

But the big Catch 22 is that when men use an interactive management mode or are trained to do it, this is seen as highly admirable. But when women do it, it is something attributed to gender and not valued! You can't win.

Reading about these leadership styles made sense of things I had experienced when I was in government. As Minister of Justice, I remember when my gun control legislation passed by a very significant majority. Gun control is a very divisive issue here in Canada. It is not quite the same as in the United States, where you have a serious constitutional provision that claims to give you the right to carry a handgun in your glove compartment. But it is very contentious in Canada, and I knew that when I decided to introduce legislation on it.

If I had simply walked into the caucus with my fellow members of Parliament and said, "This is the bill and we are going to pass it," I would have been dead at the start. It took a considerable amount of strategizing, knowing when to push, when to move out, when to time the legislation, how to create common ground in the House through consultation, listening, etc. As a result, the bill passed by a majority.

The press decided, however, that I must have somehow watered down the bill. They could not believe that my legislation had actually passed. For years I couldn't understand why they didn't give me the credit for taking this difficult legislation through. Then I read Judy Rosener's book and I said, "Aha!" The noises that I made were not the noises that the press expected from a leader. They expected me to come out to the scrum outside the House of Commons and say, "This is the bill. It's going to pass, no matter what!" If I had taken that leadership approach, my bill would have died.

So it was a very interesting insight for me that mine was in fact an effective and appropriate style of leadership. I didn't have absolute power nor should I have had. Just because I was Minister of Justice didn't mean I should be empowered to impose my personal views on the Canadian House of Commons. There was a fair process and a lot more contention in Parliament than people realized.

Gender and Communication

Another area of research that I find very helpful in understanding my own political experience is the research on gender styles of discourse. There are a number of scholars who work in this area; perhaps one of the pioneers is Deborah Tannen of Georgetown University in Washington. Her famous book, *You Just Don't Understand,* looks at gender styles of discourse in relationships. She also wrote a wonderful book called *Talking Nine to Five,* where she takes the issue into the workplace.

In her work, Deborah Tannen argues that women tend to be socialized to emphasize the rapport aspect of speech, whereas men tend to be socialized to emphasize the hierarchical aspect of speech. Again, this is not good or bad, it is simply a reality that she has observed.

The different forms of speech may go back to hunting and gathering societies, where men were out chasing the wild boar and needed to know who was where. There had to be a certain pecking order. The kinds of things that women did back then required a greater sense of equality and communal sharing.

That rapport aspect of speech may have led women to downplay their own certainty. Women are socialized to know that they will not be liked if they are too bossy, which is why women often say, "Well, you might not agree with me, but I think maybe you should such and such." Or, "Perhaps you will have a better idea, but why don't we look at so and so." A woman can be perfectly confident of what she is saying, but she is socialized to believe that she should downplay that certainty. Men, on the other hand, are socialized to emphasize their certainty. Every woman knows what it is like to be in a room listening to some man who doesn't know anything about what he is talking about but who says it so authoritatively. Where did he learn to do that? Well, it is part of his socialization.

Tannen argues that men are often reluctant to ask questions. Women, she notes, ask questions as a way to make conversation. Men usually feel that they will be in an inferior position if they demonstrate uncertainty.

So if we don't understand that there may be different styles, and if we are not prepared to look beyond speech habits, we may totally misread what someone is really thinking. One of the things that I found intriguing from Deborah Tannen's work was that I don't have the typical female way of speaking, at least the way she describes it. I don't end my sentences with a question. I don't think I underplay my

> **" GENDER LITERACY MEANS UNDERSTANDING THE KIND OF UNSPOKEN ASSUMPTIONS THAT PEOPLE BRING TO INTERACTIONS, TO TRANSACTIONS, TO THE COMMUNICATIONS OF CERTAIN PLAYERS IN THE ENVIRONMENT. "**

certainty. If I had, I don't think I would have been seen as a leader. But again, there is a "Catch 22." Sometimes I was described as arrogant. I have a lot of faults, but I am definitely not arrogant. (Trust me, believe me, I am absolutely not arrogant. I am much too wonderful to be arrogant!) I think I am respectful of other people's views and when I form an opinion I can be very straightforward in saying so. But I think when people hear that kind of certainty coming from a woman, it rankles.

This affects the way that women are perceived. You are either an irritation to the people who are observing you and interpreting you, or you are simply seen as kind of nice and sweet, but not really in the same league as those guys in the three-piece suits with the square shoulders and the deep voices who conduct themselves in a manner that everybody associates with masculinity and leadership.

Kim Fridkin Kahn has written a book called *The Political Consequences of Being a Woman.* In her research, she examines the problem of stereotypes and what it means to women in an American political campaign. According to Fridkin Kahn, women candidates actually get less media coverage than men candidates in similar elections.

She also writes about the price you pay for the different assumptions that people apply to women and men. Women are assumed not to be competent. Men are assumed to be competent. So when a man succeeds, it is attributed to competence, but if he fails it is attributed to bad luck. When a woman succeeds, it is attributed to her luck. If she fails, it is attributed to incompetence. There you have it.

If you are a success, it still doesn't dispel the stereotype. They just don't budge, those old stereotypes about women not being leaders. But, by golly, if a woman's success was attributed to her competence, maybe you would have to rethink those stereotypes. Very scary. Much easier not to do it.

So gender literacy means understanding the kind of unspoken assumptions that people bring to interactions, to transactions, to the communications of certain players in the environment. In the political arena, this understanding can empower women. Once you give names to barriers, women can actually fight against them and deal with them. And it enlightens men and enables men to be more effective partners and more effective bosses.

I think that gender literacy is a significant ethical challenge for the media. I get a chance every semester to talk to Tom Plate's Ethics and Media class at UCLA, and I say the same thing to them every time. It is not a question of checking your facts; you know you have to do that, that is basic Media 101. The real challenge, the real ethical challenge, is to try to understand the unspoken assumption, the unarticulated message, the unconscious values that you carry with you toward the people whose activities you are covering and whose actions and statements you are mediating to the public. There is a profound need for understanding.

Increase Visibility

A second way of trying to break down these stereotypes is simply to increase the visibility of women leaders. I chair an organization called the Council of Women World Leaders. Until the death of Madam Bandaranaike last week, there were 29 living women who had been president or prime minister of their country. There are now 28. Most people could name very few. You remember Margaret Thatcher, maybe Mary Robinson, but most people can count the women leaders they know on the fingers of one hand.

I had a very exciting experience recently when I was in Istanbul. I was bargaining for a carpet and the Turkish fellow who was with me to make sure that I didn't get totally ripped off happened to mention to the people in the store that I had been the prime minister of Canada. I assumed that as in most places, this would just go over their heads. But, they were very excited because, in fact, I became prime minister of Canada the same day that Tansu Ciller became the first woman prime minister of Turkey. So my picture was in all the Turkish newspapers, and they all got very excited and wanted to have their picture taken with me.

But most people don't know who these women leaders are because they tend to fall off the table once they are out of office. They are seen as an anomaly. In another example, last weekend I was in Miami as a guest speaker at the International Women's Forum where they were inducting two women into the International Women's Hall of Fame — Gloria Estefan, a very intelligent, thoughtful and interesting woman, and Hanna Suchocka, the first woman prime minister of Poland. It was very clear in the room where I spoke that only about three other people knew who Hanna Suchocka was. Once the video had been played and people understood who she was and what she had accomplished, she had a fan club. People were blown away by this extraordinary woman. But, nobody would have known her otherwise, even though the audience was a group of women who considered themselves pretty aware of powerful and important women.

> **WE WANT TO MAKE IT SO THAT A WOMAN CAN GO OUT THERE AND DUKE IT OUT IN THE POLITICAL ARENA WITHOUT CARRYING THE BURDEN OF HER GENDER.**

These women world leaders are not known and yet, if you look at their careers and their actions, their behavior while in office should dispel the stereotypes of women not being able to govern in a crisis and not being able to make tough decisions. Like her or not, Margaret Thatcher knew exactly what she wanted to do during the Falklands war.

I was a graduate student in England in the early '70s when people could only have the power on for nine hours every day. No British government had been capable of taking on the miners' union, which really was totally out of control. Not only did Margaret Thatcher take them on and defeat them, but she did it in a very strategic way. She didn't do it the first time out. Why? Because there were no stockpiles of coal. She bided her time until millions of tons of coal had been set aside and the next time she just saw the union to the finish and that was the end of it. You can like Margaret Thatcher or hate her, but a weak leader she was not.

Violeta Barrios de Chamorro defeated Daniel Ortega in Nicaragua and dealt with the extraordinary circumstances of trying to bring a country together after a civil war. The division was a personal one in her case, since her children were divided by political beliefs. Half her children were Sandinistas; the other half opposed them. De Chamorro brought them around her dinner table every week and sent a symbol to the people in Nicaragua. The message: If she can create civil relations among her own children, she can do the same for our country.

It took enormous courage and vision on de Chamorro's part to find the story, find the image, find the symbol the country needed to hang on to in order to hope for a better life.

In Poland, a woman was chosen to lead during a difficult period of economic reform. The new woman president of Latvia is undergoing an interesting process of dealing with the post-Soviet transformations, a challenge given the fact that the capital has a majority of Russians.

Corey Aquino did a great deal to help restore democracy to the Philippines. President Kumaratunga, the current president of Sri Lanka, just barely survived an assassination attempt. She is now living almost confined to her house, but she has never yielded in her determination to find a peaceful resolution through power sharing with the Tamils. She has put her life on the line for what she believes is the only way to permanently resolve the civil war in Sri Lanka.

There are many other examples, but still there is a tendency to gloss over women's careers and just see them as aberrations. The Council of Women World Leaders was created not simply to provide an opportunity for us to get to know one another and share our experiences with scholars and others interested in learning how we dealt with the challenges of our offices. It was also created to provide visibility for women rising in the political ranks, to make the notion of women leaders normal, natural, not exotic, just ho hum.

We want to make it so that a woman can go out there and duke it out in the political arena without carrying the burden of her gender. Not all women will be successful. Not all women will be great leaders. Not all men are great leaders.

The latest *Fortune* magazine has a cover story about the 50 most powerful women in business. This is great profile, but we need to move from anomaly to normality. When women do get a chance to show what they can do, it is so important to make them visible and to attack the stereotypes.

Enlightened Men

Finally, I must now dispel some stereotypes about leadership by men. Without their support, many women would not have the opportunity to lead. Many women leaders will tell you of the support they received from enlightened men. In my own career, Prime Minister Brian Mulroney appointed me to the cabinet. He made me the first woman justice minister in Canadian history. He made me the first woman defense minister in Canadian history. And he appointed a record number of women in government as ambassadors and to senior positions within the public service.

When we have the power, as women, we must seize the opportunity to advance other women. Appointing women to positions of responsibility can be hugely effective in breaking those barriers. In the past, tokenism made many successful women unwilling or unable to champion others. If there is only going to be one woman partner in the law firm, it doesn't create a great incentive for all the women in the firm to gather in support of one another.

When we get beyond that, it frees us up to be who we are, to speak in our own voices, and to reach out to other women. I remember when I was a teenager, people would say, "You're the smartest girl I have ever met. You're really smart for a girl." And I have to tell, I was flattered by that. I was in my twenties before I suddenly realized, hey, this is no compliment!

I think it is so important that when you have the opportunity to use your position to make a difference, you should.

I just want to give you a very brief example of a recent incident that underlined to me the opportunity that I have to use the cachet of my former political offices to good purpose. I was invited to speak in Bahrain to the Arabian Society of Human Resource Management. Now, I got the invitation and thought, "What is this about"? The Society is based in Saudi Arabia, but nobody has conferences in Saudi Arabia. Not a lot of fun having a conference in Saudi Arabia.

Bahrain, on the other hand, is very different. Women don't wear veils, it is very open, and women can work alongside men. The conference was on information technology for human resource management. Why was I invited? Canada for six years has been number one on the U.N. quality-of-life index, and people thought that Canadians probably had something to say about human resource management.

So what was I going to speak about? I wanted to use the opportunity to support women if I could. Well, I did some research on women in the labor force in the Persian Gulf and discovered that, in fact, there was an interesting development. In Bahrain both the prime minister and premier had been supporting women, 23 percent of their labor force was female, 35 percent in the public sector, 18 percent in the private sector. In Saudi Arabia, where less than 10 percent of the labor force is female, the crown prince of Saudi had actually gone to the U.N. in September and signed the Convention for the Elimination of Discrimination against Women.

In this small way, he was trying to send a signal about the need for some changes.

So I called my speech "Women, Information Technology and Human Resource Management." I focused on the fact that women were an increasing part of the Persian Gulf labor force and praised existing leaders for making sure that happened. I discussed gender literacy as a way for human resource managers to get the most value from their women employees and talked about the issues we face in the United States and Canada. I also discussed the rapid growth of women entre- preneurs in the United States and Canada and the impact that had on local employment. That got their attention.

I told them that women-owned businesses in Canada hired more people than the top 100 businesses in the Canadian Business magazine roster, and that in the United States women-owned businesses hire 35 percent more people than all of the U.S.-based Fortune 500 companies hired worldwide. Let me tell you, that got their attention. And I spoke of the role that information technology could play

> " **DIVERSITY CHANGES THE CULTURE OF POWER. THE EMPOWERMENT OF WOMEN HAS CHANGED THE PUBLIC POLICY AGENDA.** "

in leading the Persian Gulf women to meet these women and create partnerships. I urged them to encourage their membership to develop the business capacity of these women.

My speech was well received by both men and women but what was most important was that, as a former prime minister, as a former defense minister of a G7 country, I couldn't be dismissed. They couldn't just say, "Oh well, this is just some person talking a line." They had to take me seriously. In fact, they were very wel- coming, treating me like a man and letting my titles almost supercede my gender.

I think what was important, too, was that I was able to support local leaders by giving them pragmatic reasons for continuing cultural change. It is important when you have those opportunities to use them, as Madeleine Albright has done so effectively in making the rights of women an integral part of American foreign policy. She is not apologetic about it, women are not a minority group, America stands for this.

Democracy and Women's Leadership
Democratization is also an ally for emerging women leaders. I co-chaired a Forum

for Emerging Democracies in Yemen last year and was amazed to see that the participation of women was a fundamental principle within their definition of democratization. At the final session, the president of Yemen threw away his notes and said live on Yemen television: "We have to make the goals of this conference a reality and that includes the political participation of women." Yes, there were rumbles of discontent at one end of the hall, but the next week he doubled the number of women on the executive body of his party and gave another similar speech.

Unfortunately, as the Yemeni ambassador to the United States told me, when they rebroadcast the speech on Yemen television, they cut out the part about women, but two out of three ain't bad.

Secretary General Kofi Anan has made it a priority to appoint women to top positions in the U.N., although there are only about seven or eight women ambassadors representing their countries.

Juan Somavia, the new secretary general of the ILO has, for the first time, put women on the governing council. An eleven-member governing body now has five women. He took a lot of heat for that, too. But that kind of leadership can make an enormous difference. And, of course, President Clinton has made key appointments of women.

So why does this issue of women in leadership matter so much to me? Well, it is not a question of one gender being better than another. (Although there is a recent study from the University of Maryland suggesting that when you have critical masses of women in business and government, you get less corruption.)

What is more important is that diversity changes the culture of power. The empowerment of women has changed the public policy agenda. Issues that used to be marginalized — like domestic violence — are now in the mainstream, and they are important issues for all people.

I remember that when I brought legislation on sexual assault into the House of Commons in the early 1990s, many men stood up and gave very sensitive speeches about the terrible fear of sexual assault on the part of women. Ten years earlier, I don't think they would have made those kinds of speeches, but the presence of women and the mainstreaming of women's issues changed the culture of power. And the results were better legislation, fairer legislation, and a more democratic legislative outcome.

There is an important link between international norms and domestic policies. When we have fair treatment of women set in domestic policy, it also supports the change of international laws. The international laws then became what women look to in other countries to support their efforts to change domestic legislation. It is all of a piece.

In March 1997, an article on the front page of the *Wall Street Journal* said when symphony orchestras auditioned musicians behind a screen, they hired 35 percent more women. Unfortunately you can't run for public office behind a screen. Merit is not always recognized, and so we have to tackle the barriers. Women who have something to offer must be given a chance to offer it.

KIM CAMPBELL served as Canada's nineteenth and first female prime minister. Trained as a lawyer and political scientist at the University of British Columbia, Vancouver, and the London School of Economics, she previously held cabinet portfolios as minister of state for indian affairs and northern development, minister of justice and attorney general, and the minister of national defense and veteran affairs. From September 1996 to September 2000, Ms. Campbell was Canadian consul general in Los Angeles. In the spring of 2001, she became a fellow at the Center for Public Leadership, John F. Kennedy School of Government, Harvard University.

Managing in a World That is Round

BY FRANCES HESSELBEIN

FIVE HUNDRED YEARS AGO, RENAISSANCE MAN DISCOVERED THAT the world was round. Three hundred fifty years later, Organization Man developed the practice of management. But as this practice evolved, he forgot that his world was round, and he built a management world of squares and boxes and pyramids. His world had a special language that matched its structure: the language of command and control, of climb the ladder, of top and bottom, up and down.

In every large organization for the next 100 years, rank equaled authority. And for the most part, the old hierarchy that boxed people and functions in squares and rectangles, in rigid structures, worked well. It even developed the famous pyramid with the CEO sitting on the pointed top, looking down as his workforce looked up.

And then a period of massive historic change began, of global competition and blurred boundaries, of old answers that did not fit the new realities. In all three sectors of public, private, and social organizations, there grew a new cynicism about our basic institutions. With government, corporations, and voluntary or social sector organizations trying to ride the winds of change, a different philosophy began to move across the landscape of organizations, and with it came a new language, a new approach, and a new diversity of leadership.

In the 1970s and 1980s, some leaders in the private and the voluntary sectors saw that the hierarchies of the past did not fit the present they were living or the future they envisioned, so they took people and functions out of the boxes and, in doing so, they liberated the human spirit and transformed the organization.

Today we begin to see the new leaders, the leaders of the future, working in fluid and flexible management structures; and we hear a new language from these leaders—they understand the power of language.

"Mission-focused, values-based, demographics-driven."
"Learning to lead people and not to contain them."
"Management is a tool – not an end."

"Followership is trust."

We hear corporate leaders using more felicitous and inclusive language. For example, Jack Welch of General Electric: "Ten years from now, we want magazines to write about GE as a place where people have the freedom to be creative, a place that brings out the best in everybody, an open, fair place where people have the sense that what they do matters, and where that sense of accomplishment is rewarded in both the pocketbook and the soul. That will be our report card." A powerful corporate leader speaking of soul? The times *are* changing.

From my own experience in 1976, when I left the mountains of western Pennsylvania to begin my work as CEO of Girl Scouts of USA, the largest organization for girls and women in the world, I knew that the old structures were not right for the next decade, let alone the next century. So volunteers and staff together unleashed our people through a flat, circular, fluid management system. In the new organizational structure, people and functions moved across three concentric circles, with the CEO in the middle looking across, not at the top looking down. Five minutes after it was presented, a colleague dubbed it "the bubble chart" and

> " **WITH THE RETURN OF A MORE FLUID, CIRCULAR VIEW OF THE WORLD, THE DAYS OF TURF BATTLES, THE STAR SYSTEM, AND THE LONE RANGER ARE OVER. THE DAY OF THE PARTNERSHIP IS UPON US.** "

an observer, "the wheel of fortune." Our people moved across the circles of the organization—never up and down—and the result was high performance and high morale.

I am often asked by management students and middle managers in organizations I work with, "How can we free up the organization and make the changes you talk about if we are not at the top?" I reply, "You can begin where you are, whatever your job. You can bring a new insight, new leadership to your team, your group."

That advice applies equally—or especially—to senior executives. As Peter Senge points out in *The Ecology of Leadership* (p. 18), when it comes to sustaining meaningful change, senior executives have considerably less power than most people think. But one place where they can effect change is with their own work groups and everyday activities.

With the return of a more fluid, circular view of the world, the days of turf battles, the star system, and the Lone Ranger are over. The day of the partnership is upon us. Leaders who learn to work with other corporations, government agencies, and social sector organizations will achieve new energy, new impact, and new significance in their organization's work. But to manage effective partnerships, leaders will have to master three imperatives – managing for the mission, managing for innovation, and managing for diversity.

Managing for the mission

Understanding one's mission is the essence of effective strategy – for the small nonprofit enterprise or the Fortune 500. Consider the power of the three questions that Peter Drucker offers those who are formulating an organizational mission:

- What is our business/mission?
- Who is our customer?
- What does our customer value?

An effective mission statement must fit on a T-shirt, and it must give people a clear, compelling, and motivating reason for the organization's existence. For example, "To serve the most vulnerable," the mission of the International Red Cross, satisfies both criteria and succeeds brilliantly; "To maximize shareholder value," the de facto mission of many corporations, satisfies only the first, and fails miserably.

Managing for innovation

Peter Drucker defines innovation as "change that creates a new dimension of performance." If we build innovation into how we structure the organization, how we lead the workforce, how we use teams, and how we design the ways we work together, then innovation becomes a natural part of the culture, the work, the mind-set, the "new dimension of performance." At the same time, we must practice "planned abandonment" and give up programs that may work today but will have little relevance in the future.

Managing for diversity

Perhaps the biggest question in today's world is, "How do we help people deal with their deepest differences?" Every leader must anticipate the impact of an aging, richly diverse population on the families, work organizations, services, and resources of every community. Headlines and TV tell us that governance amid diversity is the world's greatest challenge.

Those headlines also remind us of the grinding reality that no single entity —whether public, private, or nonprofit—can restore our cities to health or create a healthy future for all our citizens. But in the emerging partnerships across all three sectors, we see remarkable openness and results. We need thousands more such partnerships. All of us are learning from one another. Thousands of dedicated public sector employees overcome daunting odds every day to improve their corner of the world. A huge social sector—with over a million voluntary organizations in the United States and over 20 million worldwide—shows what dedicated people can do, even on woefully inadequate budgets. And the incredible resources, energy and expertise of the private sector remind us that behind every problem there really is an opportunity. It is the leader's job to identify the critical issues in which his or her organization can make a difference, then build effective partnerships based on the mission, innovation and diversity to address those issues.

We need to remember that we can do little alone and yet much together. To be effective, leaders must look beyond the walls of the corporation, the university, the hospital, the agency—and work to build a cohesive community that embraces all its people—knowing there is no hope for a productive enterprise within the walls if the community outside the walls cannot provide the healthy, energetic workforce essential in a competitive world.

FRANCES HESSELBEIN is the chair of the Board of Governors of the Peter F. Drucker Foundation for Nonprofit Management and served as its founding president and chief executive officer from 1990 - 1998. She is currently the editor-in-chief of *Leader to Leader,* a quarterly publication of the Drucker Foundation and Jossey-Bass Inc. Mrs. Hesselbein was awarded the Presidential Medal of Freedom in 1998 in recognition of her leadership as chief executive officer of the Girl Scouts of the U.S.A. as well as her role in leading social sector organizations toward excellence. Mrs. Hesselbein received the ILA Distinguished Service Award at the ILA Annual Conference on November 4, 2000.

When Leadership is an Organizational Trait

By James O'Toole

INCREASINGLY, THE IDENTITIES OF CORPORATIONS ARE MERE reflections of the personalities of their leaders. Today, a business magazine won't run a cover story about the Ford Motor Company; instead, it will feature the company's CEO, Jacques Nasser, in a full-color spread. Even in the high-tech world—where one would expect the full focus of attention to be on the latest cyber gizmo—the public eye is riveted more on the persona of CEO Scott McNealy than on his company's red hot Java product—and hardly any heed is paid to Sun Microsystems as a corporation. Indeed, recent research shows that the perceived image of a high-profile chief executive brings a premium to a company's stock. Investors thus join journalists in the personification of corporations, focusing on the characters, biographies and "charisma" of CEOs. As a result, American business organizations are more often than not portrayed as shadows of the "Great Men" who sit in the chief executive's chair. In the most extreme case, for all intents and purposes, Warren Buffet *is* the Berkshire Hathaway Corporation.

And academic theory follows practice. Over the last decade, the parsing of leadership styles has become *de rigeur* in American business schools, the subject of practical (and arcane) professorial research, as well as stacks of graduate dissertations. In continuing education seminars, in MBA classes, even at the undergraduate level, professors now teach students to adopt the "right leadership style" for themselves—using "360 degree feedback" to make them aware of how they are perceived by others and, especially, to learn how to manage those perceptions. And for those who are severely leadership-impaired, there is always that growth industry called executive coaching.

This focus on personality is peculiarly American, perhaps an outward manifestation of our collective unconscious on which the image of George Washington astride his powerful, white steed is indelibly depicted. In recent times, Europeans have tried to resist such personification of leadership. Indeed, thanks to the likes of Hitler, Lenin, Stalin, Franco and Mussolini, Continental Europeans were more than happy to concede the whole sorry field of Leadership Studies to Americans after 1945. If you don't count the scads of books written in French about Charles De Gaulle, Americans owned the subject of leadership for most of the second half of the last century. And, during that time, we applied our theories not only to political leaders but, unique in the world, to leaders of business corporations.

And, of course, we got it wrong. "We" meaning those of us in American business, academia, consulting and journalism who habitually discussed, studied and wrote about leadership solely as an *individual* trait. While this obsession on a single personality is occasionally appropriate—particularly when an entrepreneur is still running a company that he or she founded—evidence offered here indicates that this perspective often skews analysis away from organizational factors which, in fact, are more important drivers of performance. My colleagues and I came to this conclusion quite by accident. In early 1999, we began a research project on strategic leadership in conjunction with the World Economic Forum. For the last

> **INSTEAD OF LEADERSHIP BEING A SOLO ACT, AN ARIA SUNG BY THE CEO, IN THESE ORGANIZATIONS IT IS A SHARED RESPONSIBILITY, MORE LIKE A CHORUS OF DIVERSE VOICES SINGING IN UNISON.**

decade, leadership sessions had been a good draw at the Forum's annual Davos conclave, but Forum members had started to grow tired of the usual bill-of-fare: a thin gruel of CEO war stories, anecdotes and homilies. Thus, we were charged with putting a little beef on the Davos leadership menu. We formed a research team and set out to create something that didn't exist: a database of hard information about the soft subject of leadership.

Working with Forum member corporations, we began our efforts with traditional premises about leaders—but soon were surprised to discover that the relative performance of large corporations cannot be explained adequately by measures of the individuals who head them. Note that operative word *adequately.* As predicted, we discovered that most of the large, global companies we studied operate, to one degree or another, under a traditional model of strong individual leadership at the top. Moreover, the quality of that leadership bears on the overall performance of those companies. But we also noticed that a few of the companies we studied—and some business units within others—are characterized by a different pattern of leadership. Instead of leadership being a solo act, an aria sung by the CEO, in these organizations it is a shared responsibility, more like a chorus of diverse voices singing in unison. Significantly, this characteristic is more than the frequently observed phenomenon of "cascading" leadership (in which a strong leader at the top empowers other leaders down the line). Although cascading is often a part of what we observed, more to the point *in these organizations many of the key tasks and responsibilities of leadership are institutionalized in the systems, practices and cultures of the organization.* Typically, cascading leadership depends on the continuing support of whoever is the leader of an organization at any given time; but what we observed is behavior that is not personality-dependent. Eventually, we realized we were observing a form of leadership that is rooted in systems, processes and culture. Without the presence of a high-profile leader (or "superiors" goading or exhorting them on) we observed that people at all levels in these organizations:

- act more like owners and entrepreneurs than employees or hired hands (that is, they assume owner-like responsibility for financial performance and managing risk);
- take the initiative to solve problems and to act, in general, with a sense of urgency;
- willingly accept accountability for meeting commitments and for living the values of the organization;
- share a common philosophy and language of leadership which paradoxically includes tolerance for contrary views and a willingness to experiment; and,
- create, maintain and adhere to systems and procedures designed to measure and reward the above behaviors.

Obviously, we did not invent this model of leadership, nor do we believe that it is necessarily new. Doubtless, it has been around a long time and we, like others, missed it because we were blinded by the powerful light that emanates from high-profile leaders. We were also prisoners of the current wisdom about the necessity for personalized, "take-charge" leadership—particularly in times of rapid change. Moreover, it is important to stress that the organization-based model we identified was not the only one we observed in our study, nor was it necessarily the most effective. In fact, the two most successful companies in our sample operate on two different models, Oracle being headed by a single strong leader, and Enron with widely diffused, and systematized, leadership responsibilities. Thus, we are not advocating a newly discovered "best way to lead." Instead, we are calling attention to a previously unnoticed—but equally viable—alternative to the traditional leadership model. Among other things, this discovery helps to explain some persistent contradictions to the dominant model of leadership: If leadership were solely an individual trait,

- Why is it that some companies demonstrate the capacity continually to innovate, renew strategies and products, and outperform competition in their industries *over the tenures of several different chief executives?* Intel, for instance, has been a rip-roaring success under the leadership of, in sequence, Gordon Moore, Andrew Grove, and now, Craig Barrett.

- Why is it that some CEOs who have succeeded in one organization often turn in so-so performances in the next? Consider George Fisher, who was a star at Motorola, but far less effective at Kodak. (Conversely, why is it that some companies headed by singularly unimpressive CEOs nonetheless rack up good performance records?)

- Why is that academics are unable to quantify the relationship between CEO style, on the one hand, and organizational performance, on the other (in fact, they have found no objective correlation between those two factors concluding, unhelpfully, that "it all depends").

Moreover, as history shows, businesses that become dependent on a single leader run a considerable risk. If that individual retires, leaves (or dies in office), the organization may well lose its continuing capacity to succeed. Witness the performance of General Motors after Alfred Sloan, ITT after Harold Geneen, Polaroid after Edwin Land, and Coca-Cola after Roberto Goizueta. More frequently, organizations learn the hard way that no one individual can save a company from mediocre performance—and no one individual, no matter how gifted a leader, can be "right" all the time. As the CEO of Champion Paper explains, "None of us is as smart as all of us." Since leadership is, by definition, doing things through the efforts of others, it is obvious that there is little that a business leader—acting alone—can do to affect company performance (other than try to "look good" to investors).

In light of the above, it should not have been so surprising that our research revealed that, in many successful companies *leadership is treated as an institutional capacity and not solely as an individual trait.* It turns out that many corporations whose familiar names perennially appear on "most respected" lists are ones with the highest institutionalized leadership capacities. Like individual IQs, companies have collective LQs—Leadership Quotients—that can be measured and compared. (Moreover, as we show below, unlike individual IQs, an organization's leadership capacity can be bolstered through appropriately directed effort). Hence, we now are better able to explain why companies like Intel, ABB, GE, Enron, BP, Ford, Nestle and Motorola continue to renew themselves year after year, and over the tenures of many different leaders. Such companies are not only chock full of leaders from the executive suite to the shop floor, they make conscious efforts to build their LQs, that is, their overall organizational leadership capacities.

That last point requires an important clarification. To our surprise, we discovered that some companies with continuing records of success do not pay much, or any, attention to traditional—that is, individual—leadership development. Instead of asking "What qualities do we need to develop in our leader?" these companies continually ask, "What qualities do we need to develop in our organization?" And, while this may seem to defy the current wisdom about the importance of leadership, on reflection it squares with experience. At Motorola, for example, there has been a decades-long pattern of self-renewal that has continually belied the predictions of Wall Street analysts who, on at least four occasions, have written the company off for dead. When it has suffered one of its periodic setbacks, how could Motorola reasonably be expected to turn itself around without a "take-charge" leader like Jack Welch at its helm? But, in fact, it has done so repeatedly, and under the collective leadership of several different individuals. In light of what we have learned from our study, we

> **THERE IS SOMETHING PALPABLY DIFFERENT ABOUT A COMPANY THAT EMPHASIZES BUILDING ENABLING SYSTEMS, VERSUS ONE THAT IS DEPENDENT ON A SINGLE PERSONALITY AT THE TOP.**

posit that the secret sauce at Motorola is its strong, institutionalized leadership capacity—systems consciously created by former CEO Bob Galvin's leadership teams over a period of thirty years.

And the effectiveness of the organizational leadership model should not come as a surprise to those who have tried to change the behavior of a CEO—or of any executive whose career has been validated by rising to the top. Powerful executives tend to see leadership as positional. To them, by definition, the CEO is *the leader* of his or her corporation. For example, a couple of years ago we suggested to the CEO of a FORTUNE 500 company that he (and his executive team) might benefit from a leadership development program. He looked at us as if we were space aliens and testily replied, "If the board thought there was someone who was more qualified to lead this company, they would have named him and not me." Given that such ego-driven denial is fairly common in executive suites, it makes practical sense that the high-LQ companies in our study focus on identifying business-related activities as the source of leadership development—that is, they stress improving the ability of their leaders collectively to do their central tasks, rather than on trying to fix them as individuals.

The lesson we take from this is *not* that individual leadership behaviors are unimportant, but that in some cases, at least, it may be more effective to treat these as secondary to organizational issues. Moreover, it is far easier for leaders to learn to do things differently in terms of business processes than it is for them to change who they are (nearly a century of experience with psychoanalysis proves that it is almost impossible to change basic individual traits, and that the rare successes come only after considerable time and effort). And it is hoped that certain leadership behaviors—as opposed to the ingrained factors we call personality—can be changed more effectively in the context of organizational and business imperatives. In our experience, individual leaders often see more clearly, and less threateningly, how they have to change personally as leaders—and why they must do so—when the reason is business-related, as opposed to personal.

Using Leadership Data as an Objective Focus for Change
In effect, our research uncovered an alternative model not only of leadership but of organizational change, as well. By surveying the behavior of over three thousand leaders at all hierarchical levels—and buttressing these with hundreds of interviews—we are in the process of creating an objective data bank about alternative ways leaders bring about strategic and organizational change. This body of data has allowed our research team to pinpoint specific business systems and processes that leaders use as levers to bring about significant shifts in organizational behavior and, ultimately, improvements in business performance. For example, at one large, global high-tech company we surveyed leaders at five different levels to collect data on sixty items related to the effectiveness of twelve categories of systems that leaders use to affect behavior.

In parallel interviews, we discovered that there were competing theories about the reasons why this company was not as profitable as its competitors. When we then analyzed the survey data, and fed the results data back to the top management team, they were able to compare the relative effectiveness of their systems to that of other companies in our study. They discovered that they did well on about eight of the key systems we measured, average on two, but that their scores for performance appraisal and decision making were near the low end of the scale. The data was unequivocal: top management wasn't holding operating heads to their commitments, and decision making was based more on relationships than on objective facts. The team, which had been in denial about some of this—and divided about what was causing the rest—was then able to come to grips with its organizational leadership problems and to create an agenda for repairing the broken systems. They also were able to identify a "concrete layer" in their hierarchy where transmission of messages from the top was getting stuck on the way down the line.

The executives then began a change process by feeding the data back to the next two levels of the organization, building consensus about the roles and responsibilities of each level, clearly identifying what needed to be done and by whom. In the process, they asked us to prepare cases of how other companies dealt with similar problems, and they discussed these in a series of four workshops over a two-month period, building a common language about, and approach to, leadership. In sum, they were able to consciously build their organizational LQ by addressing the systems that had the greatest impact on performance. The bottom line is that, by using those systemic levers, the executives became more effective change agents and leaders than had been the case in the past when they had worked with organizational development experts to alter their individual leadership "styles." They came away from the data-based exercise with the belief that, while one has to be born with charisma, they almost all could learn how to better manipulate a small set of enabling management systems. Moreover, they now had an objective way to measure the extent and degree to which the changes they had initiated had been adopted by leaders down and throughout the company.

Building Organizational Coherence and Agility

In the highest-LQ organizations we studied, leaders at all levels use such ordinary systems as goal setting, communications, capital allocations and recruiting in a conscious way in order to create two prime attributes of long-term organizational success: coherence and agility. Coherence means that common behaviors are found throughout an organization that are directed toward the achievement of shared goals. And agility is the institutionalized ability to detect and cope successfully with changes in the external environment, especially when such changes are difficult to anticipate. Until recently, scholars had posited that companies with high levels of coherence were "built to last," and that the task of leadership was to get the right fit, or alignment, among key institutional characteristics. But we discovered that not all institutional coherence is good. For instance, bureaucratic alignment anchored in the habits of the past is deadly, as we documented in a couple of the companies we surveyed. Similarly, while agility often has been identified with corporate success, we found that too much of that good thing leads to chaos and wasting resources on duplicate efforts.

What we found is that organizations need to be coherent and agile at the same time. In fact we discovered that the operating systems of high-LQ companies were not only directed to those two ends, *but that leaders viewed their prime task as creating those attributes.* (These quantitative findings from our survey are consistent with recently espoused qualitative theories about the centrality of organizational "alignment and adaptability" offered by such scholars as Harvard's Ronald Heifetz, Stanford's Charles O'Reilly and Columbia's Michael Tushman.) Significantly, one of the highest-performing companies in our study, Enron, actually aligns around agility: that is, they rigorously measure and reward the seemingly loose entrepreneurial behaviors of market responsiveness and risk-taking. In essence, Enron creates organizational coherence around shared business objectives while simultaneously encouraging the agility to meet discontinuous threats and opportunities. More specifics about Enron below, but first we should address some points of natural skepticism likely to arise concerning our approach and findings.

A Distinction with Consequences

Does it make any real difference whether leadership is treated as an institutional capacity or as an individual trait? Because fundamental premises drive behavior, when leadership is thought of as an organizational trait, there are profound consequences for almost everything that follows. For example, because ABB views leadership organizationally, its highly respected former CEO, Percy Barnevik, could "retire" at age 54 in full confidence that the company had the capacity to carry on successfully without him (thus freeing Barnevik to take on even greater responsibilities for the Swedish Wallenberg family, ABB's largest shareholders, and allowing the company to make several needed changes in structure that had been closely identified with Barnevik's tenure). Because Intel sees leadership as an organizational trait, the company did not miss a beat when Andy Grove retired as CEO—in fact, it was well-positioned to move on to a higher level, with the capacity to take on new strategic challenges. How often is it that a company not only doesn't go into the tank when a CEO as respected as Grove steps down, but actually renews itself with a fresh line of products and promising new areas of business? And the reason for the successful handoffs at ABB and Intel is not simply good succession planning. The key factor is that neither company is dependent on any one, two or half-dozen key individuals for its ongoing success. As observers note, neither company talks much about individual leadership at all. Instead, they focus on building the human capacity to manage the systems that, in fact, are at the heart of their respective successes. And that is what we found at our high-LQ companies.

The Role of Enabling Systems

In essence, we found that there is something palpably different about a company that emphasizes building enabling systems, versus one that is dependent on a single personality at the top. Since the contributions of every leader are seen as important, there is concerted effort to define and measure leadership behavior down the line—and parallel emphasis on accountability at all levels for how the enabling systems are used—and to make certain that they are used. But what do we mean by enabling systems? Here are four examples of such systems and how the high-LQ companies we studied use them in order to institutionalize leadership.

Goal setting and planning.

Some of the companies we studied religiously institutionalize the process of setting challenging goals to drive performance. While it often has been remarked that great individual leaders constantly challenge and stretch their followers, we discovered that institutions also can do this through the use of disciplined organizational processes. In several of the companies we studied, there were formal mechanisms that insured that leaders at all levels and at all times have a clear sense of how the organization is doing relative to its goals. Moreover, individual leaders are rewarded (and, yes, punished) based on rigorous measurement of performance against goals. While most organizations pay lip service to setting stretch goals—and to measuring the things that are most important to the success of their business—we found that a few rare companies actually do it, and stick with it, no ifs, ands or buts. This was an especially welcome finding because, in the personality-based organizations we studied, the punishment of poor performers either didn't happen or, when it did, it was seen as a sign of "the boss" playing favorites. But in the most structured and disciplined of the processes we observed, there is a high degree of involvement in goal setting, and highly participative processes of establishing performance metrics—thus insuring a climate of organizational fairness previously associated only with the actions of an unusually trustworthy leader.

Risk Management.

Perhaps the most surprising finding in our study was the importance of risk-management systems in creating a sense of leadership down the line. In some companies, we found formal processes designed to make certain that everyone understands the size, and likelihood, of the key risks facing the business. In light of this knowledge, leaders at all levels become willing and able to take prudent risks, and they are enculturated to (and rewarded for) avoiding negative financial surprises. Because processes (not personalities) are paramount, capital allocation is seen as an objective process of pursuing business objectives (rather than personal agendas). Thus people are confident not only that objectively defensible projects will be funded, but that the system behaves fairly when making all capital allocation decisions.

Communications.

There is a striking consensus among scholars and practitioners about the centrality of communication to the role of the leader. Significantly, we found some companies where this important task was viewed to be the responsibility of every leader at every level—and that they were evaluated on how well they performed this task. In companies where leadership is institutionalized, we found that leaders at all levels spend a significant amount of time communicating the big picture—the vision, strategy, mission and purpose of the organization. At the operating level, leaders provide ready access to information that others need to do their work. In particular, we found that those who have the most relevant information have the greatest impact on decisions.

Recruiting.

All companies recruit. But in high-LQ companies, recruiting is a prime task not of the HR department, but of operating managers at all levels (including the CEO). These companies make a conscious effort to define selection criteria for new recruits that are closely related to overall corporate goals. Some, like sports teams, even recruit "the best talent available regardless of position," instead of looking to fill specific niches. Moreover, they consciously include leadership criteria in their recruitment profiles. For example, they look for people who are interested in developing subordinates and who see leaders as teachers rather than bosses.

Different in Countless Ways

While the above may sound familiar, what is striking is that none of the companies we studied stresses all twelve of the systems we identified. Instead, they each focus on managing a few systems tightly, while leaving the others loose. For example, one high-performing corporation keeps tight control of vision and communications, but they leave it to their business units to make decisions relative to structure, recruitment, planning and the rest. Significantly, we found no pattern in the choice of systems that are stressed, and no correlation between performance and the systems emphasized. What seems important is that there be a clear focus on any two or three key systems—the particular choices being driven by the strategy, industry, or challenge faced by the company. As noted above, the two highest-performing companies in our sample are exact opposites of each other (Oracle has a traditional leadership model, and Enron is a high-LQ company), and they each emphasize quite different systems. Yet, these two dissimilar organizations are mirror images of each other in making clear and conscious choices to stress certain systems—and then disciplining themselves to following through with the application of those systems.

When all of the sixty-plus variables in our study are analyzed—the regressions run, the variations standardized, and the chis squared—what the highest-performing companies seem to have in common is that they consciously choose what systems to emphasize. Leadership is thus a rational and analytical process, and not a natural trait with which some fortunate few are born. Related, when the highest-performing companies we studied create a system, announce a major managerial policy, or introduce a change in process, *they stick to it in a disciplined way, and hold leaders at all levels accountable for behaving consistently with the chosen course.* In contrast, the lower-performing companies we studied are often characterized by arbitrary policies, inconsistent enforcement of systems, and the lack of follow-through in both implementation of policy and change initiatives. We found the above to be as true for companies, like Oracle, that operate with a traditional model as it is for those, like Enron, where leadership is institutionalized.

The Moral Equivalent of Individual Leadership

With specific reference to the high-LQ companies we studied, we think they may have developed the moral equivalent of great, individual leadership. While having a Larry Ellison, Jack Welch or Percy Barnevik at the helm is obviously desirable, and companies who have such talented leaders are indeed fortunate, such good fortune is rare. But companies with a high LQ get many of the benefits of such leadership, even if the individual in the executive suite is not a star performer. And when the individual in charge is sadly less than stellar, strong systems can help to make up for the morale-sapping effects of arbitrary, erratic, indecisive, weak or egotistic leadership. It is here that students of organizational theory will recognize shades of what Max Weber was struggling with over a hundred years ago when he advocated bureaucracy over the only alternative available at the time: personality-driven leadership. While Weber may have solved the problem of capricious and politicized management, his solution—bureaucracy—merely substituted the problems of immobility and rigidity which came to characterize not only his beloved Prussian civil service but, in time, the likes of General Motors, IBM and AT&T. But now, after a century of struggling between the Charybdis of arbitrary leadership and the Scylla of bureaucracy, high-LQ companies may have resolved the Weberian dilemma. These companies are not only both coherent and agile, they are also not burdened with the vicissitudes of arbitrary leadership.

Case in Point: Enron

Enron is a particularly instructive case of how a high institutional leadership capacity can contribute to business performance. As recently as a decade ago the company was an unlikely candidate to be chosen as *Fortune* magazine's "most innovative company" in 1999 (and, again, in 2000). In the late 1980s, Enron was a slow-growing Texas-based gas pipeline company. Today they are one of the fastest-growing, most entrepreneurial corporations in the world, moving into countless new lines of business (such as power marketing and bandwidth trading). They transformed themselves by consciously creating the opportunity for many leaders at all levels of the organization to take risks, create new businesses, and share in the fruits of their success. They started the process of change through an expensive recruiting initiative. Competing against the attractive enticements offered by high-tech companies and high-paying financial institutions, Enron successfully recruited 200 MBAs from top schools to come to backwater Houston with an unambiguous charge to shake things up.

Enron's CEO, Kenneth Lay, may not have had a detailed blueprint of what all those energetic young people would do when they got on the job, but he established an environment in which they could think creatively, speak up, try new

> " IT IS EASIER TO MOTIVATE AND REWARD LEADERS
> DOWN THE LINE TO TAKE UP THE MANTLE OF
> LEADERSHIP THEMSELVES THAN IT IS FOR A SINGLE
> CEO TO PROVIDE DETAILED DIRECTION TO HUNDREDS,
> EVEN THOUSANDS, OF MANAGERS. "

things—and motivate the existing corps of managers—all in the belief that "exposure to new talent stimulates people to do better work." And he kept it up: Enron has pursued a vigorous recruiting effort in each subsequent year. And, to build organizational coherence, the company introduced a free labor market within the company (allowing people to move around easily), and it provides training that enables them to "own their own employability." They inaugurated a policy in which there is freedom to fail without penalty if people take the right kinds of risks, and Lay gives the hundreds of new leaders Enron has recruited a free hand in running the businesses they create—and a healthy financial stake in their success. As the many leaders of Enron now say, "We are given the freedom and financial wherewithal to succeed." Not coincidentally, Enron also was chosen this year as one of *Fortune's* "ten best corporations to work for."

Lessons for the Next Generation of Leaders

A message that emerges loud and clear from our study is that CEOs like Ken Lay don't need to know all the answers, and they don't have to do all the work of leadership by themselves. In fact, Lay defined his task as creating the systems under which others would be encouraged to do all the things that typically end up on the desk of do-it-all leaders. We believe that in many, if not most, corporations, it is easier to motivate and reward leaders down the line to take up the mantle of leadership themselves than it is for a single CEO to provide detailed direction to hundreds, even thousands, of managers. To this end, it is instructive to review in passing how some of the companies in our study have used the survey data we have reported back to them. At the annual World Economic Forum meeting at Davos, Lay was joined on a panel by leaders from Oracle, Renault, and one of India's largest companies, Godrej & Boyce. They addressed common theme—the value of assessing the level of coherence and agility in their organizations, the usefulness of locating the "concrete layer" in their hierarchies where the transmission of messages to the front line get blocked, the importance of identifying and communicating the right leadership model for the organization given its particular challenges and aspirations, and the absolute requirement of pinpointing what systems should be given the highest priority in order to build the organization's leadership capacity. And all of the above is facilitated by having objective and comparable data.

Collecting and feeding back hard data about institutionalized leadership is still a new concept, and much remains to be done to make the information gathered both reliable and useful. What gives us hope that the effort is worth the candle is a comment made by a top executive in one company we studied—an organization where not all the information fed back about their leadership capacity was positive: "At least now we can discuss leadership without defensiveness. Instead of threatening egos, which is never effective, we can talk about needed changes in terms of organizational tasks. And almost everybody can buy into that process." We have found that there is nothing like a little objective data to overcome denial and to get leaders focused on the collective work that needs to be done. When top management teams work with hard facts about the effects of their collective behavior, there are *"no fits, no fights, no feuds."* Instead, they are *"amigos, together,"* in the inimitable words of composer/lyricist Stephen Sondheim.

Our message to young leaders is not that the personality-driven model of leadership is headed for extinction, nor do we believe that it should be. Clearly it will continue in small and start-up companies and in places where appeals to the human heart must be made in order to bring about drastic change that requires considerable sacrifice. (Paradoxically, the impetus to move toward the organizational model probably requires the personal leadership of a Bob Galvin or a Ken Lay, individuals willing to forego personal glory for the collective good of their enterprise.) Nonetheless, we believe that more CEOs of large companies may be drawn to the organizational model of leadership for the simple reason that it is potentially more productive and satisfying to become a leader of leaders than it is to risk trying to look like George Washington while riding a white horse.

The bad news—at least for those who like a *People Magazine* approach to business journalism—is that there may be fewer "cover-boy" CEO leaders in coming decades. The good news is that there may also be much more effective corporate *leadership*. As we now have learned, leadership need not be just a solo act.

JAMES O'TOOLE is a research professor at the Center for Effective Organizations, University of Southern California, and author of *Leadership A to Z: A Guide for the Appropriately Ambitious.*

This article is a summary of findings from a study undertaken by Booz•Allen & Hamilton and the University of Southern California's Center for Effective Organizations for the World Economic Forum. It is based on surveys and interviews conducted for that study. The author gratefully acknowledges the contributions of his Booz•Allen colleagues, Paul Anderson, Bruce Pasternack, Karen Van Nuys and Tom Williams, and his C.E.O. colleagues Cristina Gibson and Alice Yee Mark. This article also appears in *The Future of Leadership,* edited by Warren Bennis, et al (Jossey-Bass 2001).

Do Women Lead Differently?

Leadership Styles of Top Women Leaders

By Kisuk Cho

TWO YEARS AGO, I WROTE A BOOK ABOUT TWELVE PRIME MINISTERS and presidents of the world, entitled *Twelve Women Who Moved the World*. I assigned my students, who were then taking my international politics course, to evaluate women leaders' foreign policy decisions to determine if they were different from those of men.

A few days later, one of my students visited my office. She could not speak a word and her eyes were full of tears. I reflected on my lectures to figure out whether I had hurt her feelings. I finally ended up playing a little game with her. I asked her questions, and she kept on shaking her head. Did I hurt your feelings? Are you sad because of your bad grade?

I joked to make her laugh. Were you moved by my book? Her head finally went down and up and she burst into tears. I was shocked. After a pause, she started telling me her own story. She had dreamed of becoming a politician since she was very young, so she entered the political science department. Her father, however, was not only cynical about politics, but also opposed her dream. Her father kept telling her, "Why the hell would a woman want to be a politician? There are lots of better occupations out there. It's nonsense!" No wonder Korea is 85th out of 108 Inter-Parliamentary Union countries in the proportion of women MPs. Since her father persistently urged her to give up her dream, she was considering changing her major. At that very moment, she read the prologue of my book encouraging young ladies to dream of becoming politicians and offering role models. She did not leave until I assured her that I would be her strong supporter and mentor. It was one of the most unforgettable moments to me. I discovered that a professor could empower a student to be a politician.

I would like to use this opportunity to share with you my research findings on leadership styles and factors affecting leadership styles of top women leaders.

until the 1970s. Even until very recently, successful managers, in upper levels as well as in the mid-level, were perceived in terms of characteristics more commonly ascribed to men than to women (Schein and Mueller; Eagly, Makhijani, and Klonsky; Wajcman). Characteristics of masculine sex-role stereotypes are "rational," "self-reliant," "defends one's beliefs," "ambitious," and so on.

Later studies hypothesized that an androgynous person, one with a high propensity of both feminine and masculine characteristics, is a more effective manager (Powell and Butterfield). This hypothesis follows Bem's observation that androgyny and effective behavior are associated (Bem). This hypothesis was not well supported by subsequent research, however.

Numerous research findings recently attest that women "are succeeding because of—not in spite of—certain characteristics generally considered to be 'feminine' and inappropriate in leaders" (Rosener, p. 120).

Then why are we witnessing the proliferation of literature on women's leadership these days? I think one of the Kellogg Leadership Studies Projects, "Leadership in the Twenty-First Century" conducted by Drs. Allen, Bordas, Hickman, Matusak, Sorenson and Whitmire, succinctly delineated four challenges that would affect leadership in the 21st century: globalization, increasing stress on the environment, increasing speed and dissemination of information technology, and scientific and social change (pp. 41-44). Twenty-first century leadership characteristics require diversity, flexibility, interdependence, and an ability to handle complexity. These environmental changes and challenges for leadership inevitably call our attention to women's leadership, since women are believed to display feminine characteristics that are compatible with the qualities required for 21st century leadership.

A "feminine" style of leadership refers to the qualities associated with women in leadership. Whether these qualities are biologically given or socially acquired, many agree that women display traits such as "empathy, helpfulness, caring and nurturance; interpersonal sensitivity, attentiveness to and acceptance of others, responsiveness to needs and motivations; an orientation toward the collective interest and toward integrative goals such as group cohesiveness and stability; a preference for open, egalitarian and cooperative relationships, rather than hierarchical ones" (Adler; Fondas, p. 260). More specifically with respect to leadership, women are known to ascribe their power to personal characteristics like charisma, interpersonal skills, hard work or personal contacts rather than to organization stature (Rosener).

To what extent are these premises fulfilled in reality? This question pushed me to delve into the case studies of twelve women prime ministers and presidents elected by popular vote before 1993. Through this study, I pursued three questions. First, are women leaders really more feminine than men? Second, are women with a feminine leadership style more effective than others? And finally, what influences women's leadership styles or are there common denominators that give rise to feminine leadership?

Case Studies on Twelve Female Leaders

There have been about 40 female prime ministers and presidents elected or appointed since 1945. Among those, twenty received popular mandates. The top leaders included in this study are Aquino of the Philippines, Bandaranike of Sri Lanka, Bruntland of Norway, Bhutto in Pakistan, Chamorro of Nicaragua, Cresson of France, Gahndi of India, Meir of Israel, Robinson of Ireland, Peron of Argentina, Thatcher of Great Britain, and Zia of Bangladash. Although appointed, Cresson was added to the list because of her publicity and unique contribution.

Based on the case studies of the twelve leaders, I drew conclusions regarding leadership styles. Previous theoretical frameworks (Neustadt; Barber) that classify male leadership may not be appropriate for understanding female leadership. In order to test the hypothesis posed by this study, I needed to adopt a unique gender-related framework: feminine vs. masculine leadership.

Most leaders that I studied displayed abundant feminine characteristics. Aquino promised to enter politics in the place of her assassinated husband, if she got signatures from a million people. Her weak reaction to seven coup attempts, both minor and major, incurred severe criticism about her inability to control the military. But she held a conviction that cease-fires and negotiations even with guerillas would guarantee peace. She was known as a mediator of conflicts among Cabinet members. She intervened in disputes only after listening to the discussion. After leaving office, she still devotes herself to coordinating a coalition of civil organizations to solve problems in education, women's issues and poverty. Aquino clearly was effective at building consensus, mobilizing groups and leading a nation during difficult times.

Chamorro, the widow of Pedro Chamorro, defeated Ortega of the Sandinistas in Nicaragua's 1990 presidential election. Despite criticisms from male leaders in the coalition who considered her a mere symbolic leader, Chamorro appointed Ortega's brother as her commander-in-chief. This ultimately contributed to cessation of the civil war and the reduction of Nicaraguan military personnel from 90,000 to 15,000. In a now-famous story, Chamorro is seated with her two daughters and two sons for Sunday dinner, even though the siblings belonged to opposite sides during the civil war.

In Ireland, Robinson did not remain the symbolic figure, which Ireland's constitution stipulates. She was a master of communications, using symbols and gestures. For example, she kept a light on in the president's residence every night to show a warm heart to Irish immigrants scattered around the world. She reached out to Irish Republican Army spokesperson Gerry Adams, the president of Sinn Fein, as well as Britain's Queen Elizabeth. These actions are examples of feminine traits and leadership qualities.

We can also observe the masculine nature of women leaders. Thatcher is seen as a politician who utilized her gender to the utmost. She effectively captured attention in international meetings dominated by male leaders by wearing feminine suits or colorful dresses. Her leadership style, however, was masculine due to her decisiveness, firmness and aggressiveness in attacking Argentina during the Falkland War and in negotiating with labor unions.

Meir, the founding mother of Israel, is famous for her motherly leadership style arising from her informal communications and meetings in her kitchen. But

> **" WOMEN ARE BELIEVED TO DISPLAY FEMININE CHARACTERISTICS THAT ARE COMPATIBLE WITH THE QUALITIES REQUIRED FOR 21ST CENTURY LEADERSHIP. "**

she also played an assertive leadership role during several wars. Cresson, engrossed with Resistance, performed assertive leadership in promoting national interests, especially on the issues related with European integration and trade disputes with Japan.

Gandhi grew up in a politicized atmosphere. Her father, Nehru, is the father of Indian independence, and her mother fought for national independence. Indira's stubbornness and uncompromising attitude were caused by childhood traumas, including the imprisonment of her family and the loss of her mother at a young age. In spite of economic hardship, she pushed to develop nuclear weapons and promoted economic development through authoritarian leadership. Moreover, she took severe and repressive measures against ethnic and religious dissidents. She abandoned hundreds of Sikhs to be massacred at the Golden Temple. Consequently, she was assassinated by two of her Sikh bodyguards.

Bhutto, a daughter of the former prime minister executed by a military coup, endured unbelievable pain and difficulties. When she finally came to power, she was criticized for relying only on close allies and for her husband's misuse of power and corruption. She was uncompromising and distrusted others, although she actively promoted women's rights.

Brundtland and Robinson also revealed masculine characteristics. Brundtland was called a dictator when she oversaw the publishing of the "Our Common Future," which included the phrase "sustainable development." She urged developed countries to give aid to Third World countries to preserve the environment. Robinson vigorously fought against the conservative Catholic culture in order to pass a law granting women the right to use birth control.

It appears that Thatcher, Bhutto and Gandhi demonstrated typical masculine leadership styles, while Aquino and Chamorro showed a feminine style of leadership. Brundtland and Robinson have revealed a balance of both sides. Bandaranike, Peron and Zia were difficult to evaluate because insufficient information was available, and they failed to accomplish major successes.

I used a survey of 60 students to identify leadership styles. They read the biographies of these twelve female leaders. Without prior discussion on femininity or masculinity, students were asked to classify all the leaders using a ten-point scale. Although it was not perfect, we were able to classify leaders with continuous measures of masculinity and femininity using mean scores of the survey results as presented in Table 1 (see page 41). It is interesting to note that the results closely match my own subjective judgment, except for Brundtland. Students gave her a higher femininity score than I did.

As an alternative, an androgynous classification could be useful, in which masculinity and femininity comprise independent dimensions from each other, as Bem earlier designed and validated (Bem). I believe that both Robinson and Brundtland aptly fit in the androgynous type, which I call an integrated model. Integrated model refers to androgynous leadership that carries out tasks efficiently and assertively with consensus building by encompassing both feminine and masculine qualities.

Leadership Effectiveness

The second issue, which is as important as the leadership style, is the effectiveness of leadership. It is not an easy task to objectively assess leadership effectiveness. Effective, competent leadership has been identified with masculine characteristics by both men and women (Lipman-Blumen, 1996). The evaluator's gender influences perceptions, which makes neutral and fair judgment difficult to attain (Eagly et al.; Brenner, Tomkiewicz, and Schein; Wajcman). Further, previous indicators that measure leadership success should not be employed. Feminist theory has a totally different perspective in evaluating leaders' accomplishments. Traditional measures include the length of leaders' reign, whether they are reelected, and how much national economic growth has been achieved. From a feminist perspective, however, questions as to whether leaders brought peace, narrowed the gap between rich and poor, and provided special care for disabled or alienated groups, should be important considerations. In fact, feminist perspectives pose a great challenge in any empirical analysis (Groot and Maynard).

The length of a leader's reign can be viewed as an indicator of the leader's motivation to seek power, which can be inferred as a masculine trait. Bandaranike, Gandhi, Thatcher, Brundtland and Bhutto served more than one term. Peron, Bhutto and Zia were not able to finish their terms. This indicates that effectiveness of leadership is not related to gender characteristics, contrary to traditional beliefs. When we evaluate leaders' policy from feminist perspectives, Gandhi and Thatcher are regarded as leaders who dismissed women's issues altogether or ignored the needs of disadvantaged groups.

" INTEGRATED OR BALANCED LEADERSHIP IS MORE SUCCESSFUL THAN EITHER MASCULINE OR FEMININE LEADERSHIP. "

Except for a few, most female leaders displayed feminine characteristics. It is interesting to note, however, that Robinson and Brundtland are commonly cited as the most successful leaders by the students who participated in the classroom survey. They are also considered to possess characteristics of transformational leaders. They are characterized as being assertive, decisive, and competent, as well as being caring, egalitarian, and warm.

I can tentatively conclude from this study that integrated or balanced leadership is more successful than either masculine or feminine leadership. As long as female leaders compete with masculine leaders, they will not thrive if they retain only feminine characteristics. As Kulke (1993) aptly puts it, "the position of such 'difference feminism' runs the risk of establishing a new metaphysics of gender differences." While, in the past, masculine leadership characteristics were favored over feminine traits, I conclude that leaders cannot exert effective leadership without a feminine component. In sum, feminine leadership traits are just as valuable as masculine ones.

Variations in the Leadership Style

What accounts for variations in leadership style? I investigated the association of all the relevant variables with the emergence of women leaders and women's leadership styles. Variables are individual as well as structural. Individual variables include the leader's age when first in office, socio-economic background, educational level, and political ideology. Structural variables are the forms of government; geographical, cultural and historical context of the country; and level of economic and political development.

In viewing the emergence of women's leadership, diversity seems to be the rule rather than the exception. In spite of these diversities and variances, I was able to identify three common elements among top women leaders. First, most of the women leaders researched are from the upper or upper-middle class, except for Peron, Meir and Thatcher. Considering that Thatcher's class was lifted up by her marriage to an affluent man, individuals' economic backgrounds seem important for women in order to overcome the initial gender barriers.

Second, most of the women leaders received higher education except for Peron and Meir. Brundtland was a doctor and Robinson, Cresson and Thatcher received doctoral degrees. Statistically speaking, 30.4 percent of top women leaders received doctoral degrees, compared to 15.2 percent of their male counterparts. Half of my samples were educated in foreign countries and were fluent in more than one language. This prepared them to be global leaders. Robinson and Brundtland became high officials of the United Nations — High Commissioner of Human Rights Commission and Secretary General of World Health Organization, respectively.

Third, the most important commonality is that their countries were anticipating real political change right before they rose to the power. Regardless of their personal ideology, either liberal or conservative, they advanced to leadership positions as symbols of change. Chamorro and Aquino symbolized democracy and peace by ending civil wars and battles with guerrillas. Thatcher revitalized a sinking economy and reformed a paralyzed government dependent on excessive spending. Buhtto and Zia fought against Islamic fundamentalism. Robinson, Brundtland and Cresson pursued progressive policies.

There are two reasons why women leaders emerged in the period of change. First, women symbolize change and unity. They have not conspired with the establishment. Second, voters, who were sick and tired of corrupted establishment, were willing to take a risk by voting for a woman in a period of crisis or hardship. These stressful conditions led to excessive criticism of women's performance because of voters' high expectations and the difficult circumstances.

I also examined whether individual and structural factors are associated with leadership style and effectiveness. In terms of geography, four of the women are from European countries (Norway, Britain, France and Ireland), two are from Latin America, one from the Middle East, and the rest are from Asia, mainly from South Asia. Women leaders were scattered all over the world and came from different cultural and religious backgrounds. The nations that they represented also had various levels of political and economic development. Since both integrated leaders are from Europe, it appears that region has something to do with leadership style as well as effectiveness. A note of caution, however: The political cultures of Ireland and Norway are profoundly different.

Politically, the women leaders represented a broad spectrum. Bandaranike, Gandhi, Peron, Cresson and Meir were socialists, whereas Thatcher was a conservative. Aquino and Bhutto and Chamorro can be identified as liberals, whereas Brundtland and Robinson were democratic socialists. Again, a leader's ideology does not show any pattern with respect to leadership style. Since leaders are located in different political contexts, it is meaningless to compare their ideologies using a left-right scale.

Since Peron, Aquino and Chamorro were elected as presidents, the presidential system seems to be more conducive to feminine leaders than the parliamentary system. This implies a possible relationship between leadership style and recruitment process, which will be discussed later. It might also suggest that a presidential system imposes less strict entry barriers for political candidates. The level of political development seems related to leadership style, since purely feminine leaders are not found in societies with higher political development. This again suggests possible linkages between the recruitment process and the leadership style, especially that of females. A previous study shows that a politician's prior occupation plays a great role in the recruitment process. Recruitment of female leaders cannot be analyzed in the same framework as that of male leaders.

According to Genovese (1993), the political recruitment of female elites is different from that of male elites. An alternative classification for female elites should be developed. He proposes three routes: insiders, outsiders and surrogates. While Thatcher and Golda Meir are insiders, Robinson and Bruntland are identified as outsiders. Gandhi, Aquino, Chamorro and Peron, who were widows or whose power was transmitted from their fathers, can be classified as surrogates. In the case of surrogates, however, I think we need a more detailed classification on the basis of their political education.

After all, the differences in the leadership style vary with the recruitment process, which in turn determines where and how a person receives her political education. If a woman reaches the center of power from inside the political circles, as Thatcher did, she would have a higher probability of acquiring the culturally dominant masculine leadership traits.

On the other hand, in the case of outsiders, women are more likely to show creative and flexible leadership styles. This tells why transformational leaders who have been successful in reforming troubled organizations often are transplanted. This combines both feminine and masculine characteristics. Without masculine traits, they might not have been able to advance themselves to such high positions. Since they were not socialized by male politicians, however, they could demonstrate feminine leadership.

Table 1: Feminity Scores of Female Leaders by Students

Female Leader	Femininity Scores
Margaret Thatcher	2.35
Indira Gandhi	3.83
Golda Meir	4.08
Benazir Bhutto	4.13
Edith Cresson	4.58
Maria Estela Martinez de Peron	4.92
Sirimavo Bandaranike	5.25
Begum Khaleda Zia	5.50
Mary Robinson	5.75
Violeta Chamorro	5.85
Gro Halem Bruntland	5.92
Corason Aquino	7.52

Table 2: Factors Accounting for Leadership Styles

| Leader | Age | Individual variables | | | Structural variables | | |
		Socio-economic Background	Education	Ideology	Governmental Structure	Nation's Culture	Political Development
Aquino	53	Upper	University graduate	Liberal	Presidential system	Catholic-centered, conservative	Assassination, Coup d'etat prevalent, unstable
Bandaranike	44 54	Upper	University graduate	Socialist	Parliamentary system	Gender discrimination prevailing	Ethnic conflicts, unstable
Bhutto	35 40	Upper	University graduate	Liberal	Parliamentary system	Gender discrimination prevailing	Religious and political conflicts, unstable
Bruntland	42 47	Upper-middle	University graduate	Democratic Socialist	Parliamentary system	Egalitarian, no gender-based discrimination	Highly developed western democracy
Chamorro	61	Upper	University drop-out	Liberal	Presidential system	High illiteracy rate, hostile against women's rights	Long-lasting dictatorship, coup d'etat, unstable
Cresson	57	Upper-middle	University graduate	Socialist	Parliamentary system	Egalitarian, no gender-based discrimination	Western democracy, no gender discrimination
Gandhi	49 63	Upper	University drop-out	Socialist	Parliamentary system	Stratified society, religious conflicts, gender discrimination prevailing	Political corruption, imperfect democracy
Meir	70	Middle-low	University graduate	Labor Socialist	Parliamentary system	Collective	Newly Born State
Peron	43	Low	Primary school drop-out	Populistic Socialist	Presidential system	Economically, politically unstable	Military coup d'etat, unstable
Robinson	55	Upper-middle	University graduate	Democratic Socialist (Labor Party)	Parliamentary system	Conservative, hostile to women's rights	Western democracy
Thatcher	54 65	Middle-low	University graduate	Conservative	Parliamentary system	Conservative, egalitarian	Western democracy
Zia	46	Upper	High School Graduate	Liberal	Parliamentary system	Gender discrimination prevailing	Coup d'etat, politically unstable

It is important to note who taught the women classified as surrogates that politics is important. If women are the heiresses of fathers such as Gandhi and Buhtto, then they are likely to be assertive and dictatorial leaders. In cases of widows, their educational background and personal preparation before entering politics seem most significant. Educated leaders such as Chamorro and Aquino proved to be rather successful democratic leaders, whereas Peron turned out to be a total failure. The less educated Bandaranike and Zia's leadership styles are hard to identify.

Tentative Conclusions

First, female leadership cannot be divided into two styles. Rather, an integrated model should be adopted to analyze all the possible female leadership traits empirically. Further, purely feminine leadership is not found to be superior over a masculine leadership style. Some masculine leaders are more effective than feminine ones. Instead, an integrated model of masculinity and femininity of leadership traits is more successful. A close link between leadership styles and effectiveness can be established from this study.

This study disputes previous findings that masculine leadership was favored by both men and women. It partially supports the feminine advocate model of leadership since an integrated leadership style requires femininity as an essential part. This means that the feminist theory of leadership needs to be revised to incorporate both elements of gender. So why do integrated leaders outperform either masculine or feminine leaders?

Interestingly, according to Lipman-Blumen (pp. 317-318) male corporate leaders at the higher level displayed integrated leadership. Female as well as male leaders at the middle level, however, clung to masculine leadership traits, indicating an integrated model is needed at a high level of leadership.

As long as we live in a world of competition and conflict, we might not be able to abandon masculine leadership qualities such as toughness, firmness and assertiveness altogether. It is, however, equally true that in today's rapidly changing environment we find more and more room for feminine leadership traits. I think it is our responsibility and pleasure to inspire students—regardless of their gender —to become integrated leaders. On the 20th annual meeting of ILA, I will not come alone. I will be accompanied by my students, who will have become successful politicians by that time.

REFERENCES

Adler, Nancy J. (1997). *Global Leadership: Women Leaders. Management International Review.* Special Issue, Vol.37, pp.171-196.

Allen, Kathleen E., Bordas, J., Hickman, G., Matusak, L., Sorenson, G., & Whitmire, K. (1998). Leadership in the Twenty-First Century, *Kellogg Leadership Studies: Rethinking Leadership 1994-1997.* Michigan: The Academy of Leadership Press.

Axelrod, Robert M. (1984). *The Evolution of Cooperation.* U.S.: Basic Books.

Barber, J. D. (1972). *Presidential Character.* Englewood Cliffs, NJ: Prentice-Hall.

Bem, Sandra L. (1974). *The Measurement of Psychological Androgyny.* Journal of Consulting and Clinical Psychology. Vol. 42, No. 2, pp.152-162.

Brenner, O.C., Tomkiewicz, J. & Schein, V. (1989). *The Relationship between Sex Role Stereotypes and Requisite Management Characteristics Revisited.* Academy of Management Journal. Vol.32, No.3, pp.662-669.

Cho, Kisuk. (1998). *Twelve Female Leaders Who Moved the World.* Seoul: Women's Newspaper Press, (in Korean).

Colegrave, Sukie. (1979). *The Yin and Yang of the Individual: The Spirit of the Valley.* London: Virago.

Eagly, Alice H. & Johnson, B. (1990). *Gender and Leadership Style: A Meta-Analysis.* Psychological Bulletin. Vol.108, No.2, pp.233-256.

Genovese, Michael A. (1993). *Women as National Leaders.* London: Sage Publications.

Groot, Joanna de & Maynard, M. (1993). Facing the 1990s: Problems and Possibilities for Women's Studies. *Women's Studies in the 1990's: Doing Things Differently?* Groot, Joanna de & Maynard, M., eds. Houndsmills, Hampshire: Macmillan Press.

Kulke, Christine. (1993). *Equality and Difference: Approaches to Feminist Theory and Politics. Women's Studies in the 1990s.* Groot, Joanna de & Maynard, M., eds. Houndmills: The Macmillan Press Ltd.

Keohane, Robert O. (1991). *International Relation Theory: Contributions of a Feminist Standpoint. Gender and International Relations.* Grant, Rebecca & Newland, K., eds. Bloomington, IN: Indiana University Press.

Lipman-Blumen, Jean. (1996). *The Connective Edge: Leading in an Interdependent World.* San Francisco: Jossey-Bass Publishers.

Newstadt, R. (1990). *Presidential Power and the Modern Presidents: The Politics of Leadership from Roosevelt and Reagan.* New York: Free Press.Powell & Butterfield. (1979). *The "Good Manager": Masculine or Androgynous?* Academy of Management Journal. Vol. 22, No.2, pp.395-403.

Roneser, Judy B. (1990). *Ways Women Lead.* Harvard Business Review, Nov.-Dec.

Schein, V.E. & Mueller, R. (1990). *Sex Role Stereotyping and Requisite Management Characteristics: A Cross Cultural Look.* Journal of Original Behavior.

Wajcman, Judy. (1996). *The British Journal of Industrial Relations.*(in Korean).

Colegrave, Sukie. 1979. The Yin and Yang of the Individual: The Spirit of the Valley. London: Virago.

Eagly, Alice H. & Blair T. Johnson. 1990. Gender and Leadership Style: A Meta-Analysis. Psychological Bulletin. Vol.108, No.2, pp.233-256.

Genovese, Michael A. 1993. Women as National Leaders. London: Sage Publications.

Groot, Joanna de & Mary Maynard. 1993. Facing the 1990s: Problems and Possibilities for Women's Studies. Women's Studies in the 1990's: Doing Things Differently? eds. Groot, Joanna de, Mary Maynard. Houndsmills, Hampshire: Macmillan Press.

Kulke, Christine. 1993. Equality and Difference: Approaches to Feminist Theory and Politics. Women's Studies in the 1990s. eds. Groot, Joanna de and Mary Maynard, Houndmills: The Macmillan Press Ltd.

Keohane, Robert O. 1991. International Relation Theory: Contributions of a Feminist Standpoint. Grant, Rebecca and Kathleen Newland (eds.). Gender and International Relations. Bloomington, IN: Indiana University Press.

Lipman-Blumen, Jean. 1996. The Connective Edge: Leading in an Interdependent World. San Francisco: Jossey-Bass Publishers.

Newstadt, R. 1990. Presidential Power and the Modern Presidents: The Politics of Leadership from Roosevelt and Reagan. New York: Free Press.

Powell & Butterfield. 1979. The "Good Manager": Masculine or Androgynous? Academy of Management Journal. Vol. 22, No.2, pp.395-403.

Roneser, Judy B. 1990. Ways Women Lead. Harvard Business Review. Nov.-Dec.

Schein, V.E. & Mueller, R. 1990. Sex Role Stereotyping and Requisite Management Characteristics: A Cross Cultural Look. Journal of Original Behavior.

Wajcman, Judy. 1996. The British Journal of Industrial Relations.

KISUK CHO is a professor of political science at the Graduate School of International Studies of Ewha Womans University in Seoul, Korea. She is the director of Ewha Forum for Global Leaders and the author of *Twelve Top Women Leaders Who Changed the World*. Dr. Cho's research and writings have been in the areas of elections, game theory, women's studies and Leadership Studies. Dr. Cho also has served on the editorial boards of the *Journal of Public Policy and Management*, the *International Studies Review*, and the *Korean Journal of Legislative Studies*. She earned her Ph.D. from Indiana University.

The Inner Work Of the Leader™

By Katherine Tyler Scott

IN THE PAST DECADE MANY EXPERTS IN A VARIETY OF FIELDS — business, education, social services, government and religion — have noted a seismic shift in the way in which we view the nature of reality. This paradigm shift is significantly changing the definition, pedagogy and practice of leadership.

The world view with which we are most familiar is that of the Scientific Age. In this paradigm, problems are perceived as eminently solvable and responsive to technical expertise. Procedures for problem solving are frequently documented and occasionally canonized in a culture that relies heavily on cause-and-effect thinking. The system is a hierarchical, top-down structure in which the leader is in charge. Authority is vested in those with position, and power is experienced as limited and available to just a few. The operating belief is one of scarcity and breeds competition and a hoarding of knowledge and expertise. A person's value is equated with external possessions, i.e., title, office size and location, salary, etc. In this paradigm, leadership is equated with status and external authority.

The emergent paradigm, the Relationship Age, is the seeming antithesis of the Scientific paradigm. In this view of reality, authority is dispersed throughout the organization or the system, and the leader is the first among equals. Leadership is shared, and the gifts of each individual, though not equal, are equally valued and used in the accomplishment of the work. Complex problems are perceived as adaptive rather than technical and require that those with the problem be involved in formulating solutions. Power is viewed as infinite; the more that is shared, the more that is created. This paradigm breeds a sense of abundance, inviting collaboration and cooperation and fostering a belief in the interdependence of people. A circular model of leadership prevails, and the capital in this paradigm is information. Unlike the Scientific paradigm, in which facts are seen as the sole reality, the Relationship paradigm values the *meaning* of the facts and recognizes multiple sources of truth. Creativity and innovation flourish. Trust is the capital that holds the organization or system together and enables it to retain effectiveness and integrity.

The experience of a shift from the Scientific to the Relationship paradigm causes concern in some about the value of order and structure, and whether there is sufficient accountability. The question, "Who's in charge?" is more easily answered in the Scientific paradigm. There are benefits and limitations inherent in both paradigms, but the rapid pace and complexity of change point out the need for adaptive behavior and prudent, quicker responses to problems. As leaders experience the shift to the Relationship Age, the choice we face is not one or the other, but some combination of both. The reality that most leaders experience is that these paradigms coexist. The challenge for leaders is to hold the two paradigms

" **PREPARING LEADERS FOR THE FUTURE AND** "
EQUIPPING THEM TO SEE DIFFERENTLY IS THE MOST
IMPORTANT WORK WE CAN DO. IT IS PREPARATION
THAT BEGINS WITH INNER WORK.

together, modifying and adapting appropriate elements from both. Leaders must hold the tension of the opposites together and lead change in "a time of no longer and time of not yet" (Hanna Arendt). The capacity to do this successfully requires a different understanding of leadership. It calls for perceiving the leaders as trustholders who possess the qualities and the capacities to hold individuals, organizations and communities in trust[TM1], and who have the psychological strength to deal with high levels of ambiguity and anxiety during prolonged periods of change.

The capacity to hold in trust[TM] is dependent on the completeness and wholeness of the leader. This means that while the development of technical skills will remain important, the *being* of the leader is equally consequential in exercising effective leadership. Preparing leaders for the future and equipping them to see differently is the most important work we can do. It is preparation that begins with inner work. Inner work reminds leaders of the impact their sense of self can have on the external environment. The leader who is self-aware is better able to understand self and others and uses this significant and deep understanding to be more accepting and empathic in his or her relationships. Inner work brings to consciousness the whole person; it is the integration of the visible and the invisible, the known and the unknown parts of self so that the whole, healthy development of individuals and organizations is valued. Self-awareness is powerful. Richard Niebuhr, one of the 20th century's greatest philosophers, writes in *The Responsible*

Self, "Self knowledge is no mere luxury to be cultivated during idle moments. It is essential to the responsible self." It is also essential to the responsible leader.

Inner work engenders responsible behavior and engages the leader in the process of bringing together the inner and outer realms of life so that the true self can be identified, claimed and shared. The leader out of touch with a true self will be less effective in managing the tension of the opposites and in leading others in meaningful change. Unclaimed internal disconnection can be projected onto others in ways that fragment and cause individual and organizational dysfunction. What the leader cannot own is given to others, blurring boundaries and creating an environment that makes it difficult for others to be or become whole. The leader's capacity to engage in inner work fosters an environment that permits others to discover themselves and claim their full potential. The inner work of leaders is central to their external success. It is a discipline involving ten habits of the mind and practices of the heart.

Engaging in Silence & Solitude

Solitude is one of the most important and difficult practices, for it requires a stripping away of all of the external props we use in our lives to affirm our sense of identity and worth. It is not the equivalent of privacy, as Henri J. Nouwen reminds us in *The Way of the Heart:* "Solitude is not a private therapeutic place. Rather, it is the place of conversion, the place where the old self dies and the new self is born, the place where the emergence of the new woman and the new man occurs."[2] Our busyness, titles, degrees, positions, and other external validations are given up for the while, and we encounter the unadorned soul and come to know its source and its sufficiency in our lives.

Solitude is clearly not for the faint of heart; it requires courage and belief in something greater than self or ego. It is a profoundly spiritual discipline, for what lies in the depths of our hearts is the discovery of our connection to that which is, was, and will be. It is an encounter with the transcendent, the unknown, and the unproven. Yet it is also the source of our real connection to the present, to the now, to an understanding of who we are. It is a practice that reminds us that we are part of a vastness, the recipients of a deep and profound love that is everlasting, no matter who we are or what we do.

Solitude can be terrifying when first practiced. The external reality is hard to ignore, but with persistence and patience, we can come to a place of quiet centeredness and create a space in which solitude becomes renewing and clarifying. In the encounter with nothingness, we can find the courage and peace to quiet whatever terror resides in our hearts.

"Silence is solitude practiced in action,"[3] according to Nouwen. If we can experience such solitude and allow our actions and speech to be formed from it, our words and deeds will take on a wisdom and intensity that will be valued by others.

Living the Question

Living the question is the practice of being open to inquiry and continual learning. It is cultivated through conversation and dialogue in which questions are as valued as answers. Between 1984 and 1996, I participated in two groups composed of scholars, researchers and practitioners convened by the Lilly Endowment to explore and study trusteeship and leadership. One of the most important things I learned over those years was the value of the question and its centrality not only in good scholarship, but also in good leadership. So much of interaction with others centers on generating answers rather than creating questions. Unanswered questions leave those of us who have a high need for closure feeling anxious and incompetent. Living the question is the ability to be secure enough to live without absolute certainty and final truth long enough to attain a fuller truth. It is the process of engaging in a quest, a discovery, of being open to surprises. Living the question is an open invitation to really look and see what is evolving rather than restricting ourselves to see only that with which we are familiar.

Our culture equates leadership with having the answers, but the real work of leadership is the capacity to embrace asking the question. To do this means we must acknowledge that what we know, while valuable, may be insufficient. We can begin with an "I don't understand" or an "I don't know" rather than feeling compelled to have an answer. I once saw a sign that confirms this: "It's far better to have unanswered questions than to have unquestioned answers." Good questions require depth of thought; they help us to think, to focus, to establish patterns and boundaries of inquiry, all of which can lead to productive periods of study, analysis, and meaning-making. Living the question helps us not only to see what is new and emergent, but to see what has been in a new way.

Holding in Trust™

What does it mean to hold something in trust? The answer is a deeply personal one. It is being responsible for something (or someone) that we don't possess, own, or have ultimate control over, and it is knowing that when our responsibility is completed, we will have contributed to improving the capability and health of individuals and organizations and to enhancing the conditions, in some instances, for those we may never know and for a time we may never see.

Leaders who have had the experience of being held in trust realize the gift it represents in their own lives and know that, in order to hold others in trust, they need to remember and know what it is to have been held in trust. Someone genuinely cared about them, saw their potential and nurtured it. Their care and involvement helped them to become capable, successful people. Remembering what it was like to have been held in trust reminds us of the deep sense of gratitude that resides within us for having had this experience and of our deep obligation to keep the gift moving through holding others in trust.

Knowing Your History

Knowing your history is much more than having a resume or a recitation of some other chronological form of facts or events; it is a depth knowledge of individual and corporate character and identity. It is knowing our personal and organizational stories over time and interpreting their meaning and their import. Our story surfaces our strengths, successes, challenges and difficulties and our capacity to respond to them. Stories are revelatory—they reveal incidences and evidence of service and leadership, lessons learned, challenges faced. They ultimately reveal our character, our core values and beliefs and how they were shaped. In their telling is reflected our capacity to care for and to lead others.

Knowledge of our history is also a source of inspiration and psychological sustenance, especially during times of difficult transition. It helps in summoning forth the tenacity and courage needed to move into the unknown; in order for us to access this power, our stories must be known and continually told. As Carl Dudley, professor and theologian, states, "The telling of your story is not merely repeating the past; it is bringing the past into the present for the sake of the future."[4] Knowledge of our history provides a deep rootedness that influences everything we do. We ignore or forget this at great risk.

When history is embraced, it can be the catalyst that helps us to face change with courage, to adapt to change with innovation, and to lead change with integrity.

Reading Reality Truthfully

Reading reality truthfully is the practice of taking time to observe the external—of seeing clearly what exists outside of ourselves. It is the practice of seeing contextually, of interpreting what is going on around us. It is the ability to analyze and to determine the implications for the analysis on the present and the future. Reading reality truthfully involves a willingness to dispense with psychological and intellectual blinders, to open ourselves to very different and diverse perspectives. This is a practice of reading, literally and figuratively. It involves the acquisition of information through comprehensive research, study and discussion. Documentation, observation and experience provide us with a cultural and contextual reading. The awareness and interpretation of information at this level can provide us with a perspective that can then be tested through conversation and experience. I believe one of the most needed leadership skills in the future will be the ability to read culture and to test perception.

Reading reality truthfully means that we greatly maximize our ability to observe and to listen, to anticipate changes and better position ourselves and the organizations we serve. It enables us to be flexible and effective in managing transition and change, and it teaches us to respond to situations in ways that are morally, ethically and spiritually responsible.

Discerning Your Mission

Discerning mission is a process of examining our core values and beliefs, of knowing whom we serve and what we do. Having clarity about these components provides the basis for setting a coherent direction for our lives; it anchors our choices and actions and increases our capacity to set appropriate and clear boundaries. Clarity and congruence in these ways help us to operate with integrity and centeredness as we seek to lead others.

Discerning mission is a critical practice of the heart that is, like all the practices, personal and institutional. The significance of institutional mission is eloquently captured in the words of Robert Lynn, former vice-president of religion at the Lilly Endowment. "At the root of the creative institution is a shared sense of vocation, a common calling. ... The presence of calling is embraced as a gift. The consequences of that gift are evident in a corporate sense of identity and in a unifying loyalty to a set of purposes. If that root sense of mission either has died or is decaying, the whole institution will sooner or later be affected in every respect. Nothing can be more subtle or serious an ailment than this sort of root disease. But whenever an institution undergoes renewal, its life springs from a deepened commitment to its vocation."[5] Knowing our own mission and working to clarify and connect it with organizational mission is the root work of leadership—so deep and so essential to our lives and the lives of institutions we serve and lead.

Discerning mission is a search for the significance of our lives and for congruence between our words and our deeds. When our personal mission is clear and we can see how it is related to our work in organizations and in communities, a great deal can be accomplished. When we experience burnout and chronic distress, one of the chief reasons is engagement in work that is disconnected from, or incongruent with, our core beliefs and values.

Managing the Gap

Managing the gap is the practice of living between the ideal and the real and involves the capacity to engage others and ourselves in addressing the real issues when the problems and their solutions are not clearly defined. It involves the ability to acknowledge disparity, imperfection and incongruence without succumbing to despair.

Managing the gap is predicated on the ability of the leader to manage his/her own anxiety and ambiguity and to use the accumulated wisdom and confidence derived from past experiences in mobilizing others to confront and address tough issues. Managing the gap involves managing self and others through significant transition and change. It integrates all of the practices.

In *Leadership Without Easy Answers,* Ronald Heifetz expresses the view that what is necessary to narrow the gap between the ideal and the real is not only an accurate assessment of reality (what is) and a clarity of vision (what is hoped will be), but the ability to manage high levels of ambiguity and anxiety. I concur and believe it involves mobilizing others to engage in moral reasoning and to seek substantive and effective action. This is dependent upon the capacity to live with chaos long enough to grasp what the real problem is so that appropriate and substantive responses can be developed. It is what I described earlier as "living with the tension of the opposites." To do so is to embrace the paradox created by situations. Leaders are people of paradox. Leaders are capable of projecting both light and shadow, of creating cultures of health or toxicity. Self-knowledge can diminish negative impact and nurture creative elements in a culture.

Appreciating Differences

Appreciating differences is the ability to respect and work with individuals and groups of different professional, ethnic, economic, religious and cultural backgrounds. It is respect for the dignity and worth of every human being. When we engage in this practice, we become better persons, maximize our resources and expand our choices. Biases and prejudices originate from fear, isolation and ignorance and very easily lead to constriction of choices and rigidity of perceptions. Inner work develops the capacity to appreciate difference; it contributes to expansive thinking and behavior. Those who engage in this practice know a world much larger than, and different from, their own. Such leadership is not just aware of cultural diversity, it is able to transcend boundaries and relate meaningfully to those who are different from themselves. To engage in this practice means we need to examine our own projections and prejudices so that we don't perpetuate or create hurtful divisions between people. We will screen for behavior (our own first and others' second) that is toxic and destructive to the development of community and collaboration and reframe issues in ways that draw attention to common interests rather than allow differences to degenerate into positions or personal attack.

This practice enables good boundary setting also. The leader who is capable of knowing what belongs to her and what belongs to others is going to be able to modulate the group's anxiety and place the assumption of responsibility with intention and integrity. She will see the signs of overload, displacement, projection, scapegoating, flight, work avoidance, ownership, motivation and balance and gauge her actions accordingly. It is not difficult to get others in a group or organization to do your work (that which belongs to you) for you. Side talking, mumbling, martyrdom, passive aggressive behavior—all are ways to avoid real work, to get others to be angry for you, to express discontent and frustration while you retain a desired persona. It is a way to build a bond and cohesiveness in groups, but it is dependent on having an external enemy and it keeps the group from growing, from seeing the decay within. The focus is on protection and defense, not progress and change.

When appreciating differences is practiced, the environment that created such maladaptive behavior is forever altered.

Creating Hospitable Space

Creating hospitable space is a critical practice in the effective exercise of leadership and involves the development of safe space in which a community of truth can be practiced. It is the creation of space in which we can bring our whole selves, our minds and our hearts.

The leadership challenge is to create safe spaces for people where the nurture of spirit and intellect are valued and can flourish creatively. You may already be skilled at doing this. As a leader, you will be relied upon to provide the space in which others can learn to manage the anxiety and tension between the private and public realms in their lives—a space where they can negotiate the relationship between private needs, hopes, aspirations, and demands of the larger community.

Hospitable space is so important because the inner work of leadership is higher risk and always challenging. To open yourself to significant change requires a place that honors and respects the learner and that uses conflict constructively to build rather than divide individuals and community.

This practice understands, as Parker Palmer shared in a TLD Leadership Institute, that "knowing and learning are communal acts that require many eyes and ears, many observations and experiences; that both require a continual cycle of discussion, disagreement, and consensus over what it all means."

Regardless of whether the setting is professional or communal, this skill is important in your exercise of leadership. The creation of hospitable space brings people together in a discovery of a fuller truth and releases the forces necessary for the healing of mind and heart.

Claiming Your Authority

Claiming your authority calls for the conscious acknowledgement of your own power and the capacity to influence. It is informed by your knowledge of the derivation of that power and influence. If you have power and refuse to acknowledge that you do, it is difficult, if not impossible, to use it constructively. The denial of power can easily lead to forms of oppression—our own and, unwittingly, those we intend to serve. The habit of claiming our own authority is an act of owning responsibility for our part in co-creating the world, of liberating our voices and finding ways to participate and make a difference in responsible decision making and policy development.

Regardless of title or position, we all have power—the capacity to influence individuals and organizations, to frame issues and determine solutions. When there is a consciousness about having power, we have the choice of exercising it with judiciousness and with integrity.

Summary

All of the practices are powerful shapers of character and behavior. The practice of leadership is profoundly connected to and grounded in them, but claiming your authority is the catalyst for transforming the journey of self-examination, self-awareness, and self-knowledge into the outer work of action.

This practice recognizes that power is the ability to affect change at the very deepest levels of our souls, hearts and minds. In the process, we transform the inner being and the outer reality, and this process begins with claiming our own authority.

Inner work is a dynamic process of self-exploration and formation that enables the leader to know self first and, in this deep knowing, to connect to others. It enables individuals to lead others — to lead in a time between times, to lead in a manner that fosters the natural desire for growth and brings about positive transformational change. Inner work is the ground for developing the authentic leader and cultivating leadership with integrity — the kind of leadership needed now and in the future.

REFERENCES

Heifetz, Ronald. (1994). *Leadership Without Easy Answers.* Cambridge, MA: Belknap Press.

Kellerman, Barbara & Matusak, L. eds. (2000). *Cutting Edge Leadership 2000.* College Park, MD: James MacGregor Burns Academy of Leadership.

Lynn, R.W. (1984). *Penetrating the Mystery of Leadership Through Depth Education, The Lilly Endowment Annual Report.* Indianapolis, IN.

Nouwen, Henri. (1981). *The Way of the Heart.* New York: Seabury Press.

Tyler Scott, Katherine. (1999). *The Inner Work of the Leader: Discovering the Leader Within.* Indianapolis, IN: Trustee Leadership Development, Inc.

Tyler Scott, Katherine. (1997). Preparing Leaders And Nurturing Trustees: Building the Capacity to Hold in Trust. *Educators' Manual.* Indianapolis, IN: Trustee Leadership Development, Inc.

KATHERINE TYLER SCOTT is the president of Trustee Leadership Development, Inc., a national leadership education center in Indianapolis, Indiana, whose mission is the development of transformational leaders with the capacity to hold individuals, organizations and communities in trust™. She has over 28 years of experience as a consultant and trainer in organizational development, leadership development and change management. Ms. Tyler Scott is a graduate of Ball State University and received her master's degree from Indiana University. She developed the Lilly Endowment Leadership Education Program and consulted with statewide and national leadership programs and designed curricula used internationally. Ms. Tyler Scott is the author of numerous publications and curricula, and a contributing author to *Spirit at Work and Stories From the Circle.* Her most recent book, *Creating Caring and Capable Boards: Reclaiming the Passion for Active Trusteeship,* was published by Jossey-Bass in February, 2000.

[1] Hold in Trust is a trademarked phrase of Trustee Leadership Development, Inc.

[2] Nouwen, H. (1981). *The Way of the Heart,* p. 27.

[3] Nouwen, H. (1981). *The Way of the Heart,* p. 44.

[4] Dudley, C. (1990). *The Trustee Educator,* Volume 1 Number 1, p. 4.

[5] Lynn, R., *Penetrating the Mystery of Leadership through Depth Education.*

Teaching and Assessing Leadership and Professional Skills

By Bonnie Pribush and Marilyn Bedford

THE FRANKLIN COLLEGE LEADERSHIP PROGRAM BEGAN IN 1991 and has, from the beginning, focused on integrating leadership content and skills throughout the traditional liberal arts curriculum. The College adopted five basic premises and a description of a leader. They are:

- Everyone has the capacity to be a leader.
- Leadership is value-based.
- Leadership can be taught.
- Leadership is best taught in context.
- The entire campus (faculty, staff, administration and students) must model and teach leadership.
- A leader is self-aware, works well with diverse people, and is willing and able to take action.

Choosing to integrate leadership throughout the curriculum requires an on-going faculty development program. Initially faculty had to be convinced that Leadership Studies was a legitimate area of study with an established body of literature. Preparing faculty to teach *about* leadership was a relatively easy task. They are by nature curious and interested in learning and so enjoyed reading and debating the theories of leadership. In the early 1990s, through a generous grant from the Lilly Endowment, an incentive structure was developed that ultimately involved nearly two-thirds of the faculty in studying leadership and teaching leadership concepts in at least one of their classes.

Campus support for the leadership program, while not unanimous, did include faculty, students, student affairs professionals, administrators and trustees. In 1998, the slogan for a more concerted, visible marketing campaign for the college became "For Leaders, For Life." Use of this slogan resulted in a serious review of the leadership offerings. Preparing students *for* leadership requires more than teaching *about* theories and examples of leadership.

History of the Professional Development Program

In 1992, Dr. Clifford Dietz, a trustee of the college, established a Professional Development Program on campus with the goal of better preparing students to function as professionals. Approximately half of Franklin's students are first-generation college students. Many of them do not come from professional families and so, in addition to subject content knowledge, they need to develop the "polish" that will set them

" TO PREPARE FOR LEADERSHIP, STUDENTS MUST PRACTICE NEW BEHAVIORS. "

apart and enable them to be more competitive in the workplace. Where the Leadership Program focuses primarily on developing citizen leaders, the Professional Development Program is concerned with skills that are useful in the workplace. In 1998, the directors of both programs agreed that it was possible to identify a common set of skills and competencies. This would make it easier to enlist faculty in teaching the skills than if there were two separate and competing lists. Also, it provided a powerful alliance between student affairs (where the professional development program is housed) and academic affairs (where the leadership program is housed).

The shift from teaching *about* leadership to teaching *for* leadership was not a trivial one, particularly for the faculty. It is no longer enough to teach content, information, facts and theories. Cognitive knowledge is still necessary but it is not sufficient. To prepare *for* leadership, students must practice new behaviors. These behaviors go beyond the sort of laboratory techniques that scientists have long taught, because they are situational.

Clearly, doing this well was going to require much internal, developmental work. Usually when faculty teach content, there is an accepted core of information. In this case, the faculty had to first agree what exactly it was that they were trying to teach. Then they had to develop techniques for teaching. Finally, they had to be able to assess whether they were having any success.

In 1998, the two directors began the work of building consensus in the campus community around a set of skills or competencies that students would need to be successful as leaders and professionals. The directors used their own experience, knowledge and resources to develop an initial list. They then met with academic departments, college administrators, the student affairs staff, the Student Congress, and other college staff members (especially work/study supervisors) in groups and as individuals. For almost a year, the directors spent many hours painstakingly gathering support for and understanding of a list of leadership and professional goals.

Some of the goals were familiar and have long been taught at the college, for example, "write well" and "think critically." Other goals (e.g., "integrity" and "commitment") may have always been hoped for results but were never intentionally taught in a way that required developing activities and assignments and assessing the results. Faculty acceptance would only come through many hours of discussion, careful rephrasing, and spirited arguments about the purpose of a liberal arts education. Finally, on November 10, 1998, the faculty endorsed the Leadership and Professional Goals. They agreed that all students at Franklin College should, in the course of their education, receive instruction and assistance in developing these skills and competencies. Hence, they also agreed that they would assume some responsibility for the instruction.

Leadership and Professional Goals

Personal Qualities

Integrity

A personal, ethical framework

Responsibility/Accountability

Personal vision and goal setting

Willingness to learn and change

Physical well-being

Commitment

Self-awareness

Interpersonal Competencies

Appreciate diversity

Give, receive and learn from feedback

Share leadership

Create a shared vision and find common ground

Work with and in a group

Manage conflict

Initiate and manage change

Communication Skills

Present ideas effectively

Read with high comprehension

Attend to non-verbal communication

Participate in and conduct civil discourse

Write well

Listen well

Balance advocacy and inquiry

Speak confidently in public

Cognitive Abilities

Solve theoretical and applied problems

Transfer knowledge and create analogies

Practice integrative thinking

Manage complexity and ambiguity

Exercise an awareness of international perspectives

Think systemically

Think critically

Think creatively

Assess and manage risk

Make decisions

At the same time, the college was preparing for its North Central accreditation visit in 2002. A part of this preparation included the development of student learning plans for departments and for the general education core curriculum. The vice president for academic affairs, Dr. Allen Berger, suggested that integration of the leadership and professional goals in these student learning plans would ensure accountability for their implementation. As a result of his leadership and the work of the General Education Council, four of the five major goals for the General Education Student Learning Plan are directly connected to the leadership and professional skill set. The next challenge was helping faculty to incorporate these goals in their own departmental student learning plans.

Supporting Faculty and Staff

To develop a plan for faculty and staff development that would focus on defining, teaching and assessing these goals, the directors of the Leadership Program and the Professional Development Program consulted with the Social Interactions Skills Department, Alverno College; Dr. John Savagian, Alverno College; Dr. Barb Bickelmeyer, Instructional Systems Technology, Indiana University; Dr. Mark Shermis, Indiana University/Purdue University, Indianapolis; and Dr. David Hendrickson, Tusculum College.

With this background, the directors developed a plan to help faculty teach and assess leadership skills. The Dean of the College offered an incentive of $1,200 in departmental discretionary funds for any academic department that had at least 50 percent of their faculty complete the entire plan. There were three requirements for participating faculty:

- Attend a full-day workshop on assessing skills.
- Attend at least one two-hour follow-up session.
- Complete a class project, including surveys and assessment.

The entire sequence of activities was offered three times: the spring of 1998, the fall of 1999, and the spring of 1999. Twelve (of sixteen) departments, thirty-four (of fifty-five full-time teaching) faculty, and five (of eleven) student affairs staff participated in the workshops, though not all completed the entire plan.

There were three goals for the full-day workshop:

- to help professors develop strategies to teach leadership and professional goals to students,
- to help professors assess student growth in these goals, and
- to help professors integrate these goals in their student learning plans.

To accomplish these goals we focused on three distinct steps: defining the skills, teaching the skills, and assessing the students' mastery of the skills.

Defining the skills

The first step in teaching or assessing is to have a clear definition of what one is attempting to teach. Many of the goals are words that are in common everyday use (integrity) and yet, much like the word leadership, there may not be a common understanding of what is meant. Modeling the way, the directors provided two definitions. Because the goal list had been built with the faculty and staff and because participation is crucial to the success of this project, the participants in the workshop were then placed in small groups to craft a definition of one of the goals. Groups were assigned to present their definitions either through a skit, musically, or visually before sharing the written definition. This activity has developed a set of definitions with community ownership. Two examples are given below.

• *Manage Conflict:* The ability to communicate and interact with individuals and groups in such a way as to handle differences, disagreements and/or more intense forms of opposition so that productive, effective solutions can be developed.

• *Work Well in a Group:* The ability to practice positive behaviors that help a group achieve a goal and that contribute toward good relationships in the group.

Even a clear definition does not provide enough of a framework to develop teaching activities and especially assessment strategies. The next question that must be answered is, "How will we know these skills when we see them?" This requires stating actual behaviors that can be observed in developmental steps as students master the skill. Again, the directors presented examples and then asked that the groups refine their definitions.

Skill: Manage Conflict

Skill Levels:
- Describe and define responses to conflict.
- Describe and recognize skills and methods for conflict management.
- Demonstrate skills and methods for conflict management.
- Facilitate conflict management between individuals and groups, valuing conflict as having constructive potential.

Skill: Work Well in a Group

Skill Levels:

- Name and define positive and negative behaviors and group stages and roles.
- Recognize group behaviors in oneself and others.
- Purposefully choose to practice positive behaviors.

Unfortunately, even this level of detail is not sufficient to develop good teaching and assessment strategies. Professors still must be able to clearly answer two questions: How would you know it if you saw it? What will the student know or be able to do? In much the same way that professors break down the information that will be acceptable as a correct answer or the type of reasoning that will receive full credit on tests, they must now define observable behaviors that confirm a student's mastery of the skill. This work was again done in groups with the directors modeling the way.

Skill: Manage Conflict: Behaviors

Level 1: Describe and define responses to conflict

- Articulate the five responses to conflict from the Thomas-Kilmann Conflict Mode Instrument.
- Define functions and dysfunctions of conflict.
- Identify root causes of conflict and possible interventions.

Level 2: Describe and recognize skills and methods for conflict management.

- Articulate options other than violence and competition.
- Articulate a problem clearly.
- Advocate a position with facts, opinions, experiences, feelings.
- Inquire respectfully into another's different perspective.
- Define "I message."
- Distinguish between "issues," "positions" and "interests."
- Brainstorm and invent options for mutual gain.
- Use objective criteria to evaluate options.
- Recognize responses to conflict in self and in others.

Level 3: Demonstrate skills and methods for conflict management.

- Demonstrate the skills listed in level 2.
- Listen with the ability to restate and summarize.
- Validate own and other people's emotions.
- Attack a problem, issue, or situation without attacking people.

- Take responsibility for self.

Level 4: Facilitate conflict management between individuals and groups, valuing conflict as having constructive potential.

- Define and distinguish between conciliation, negotiation, mediation, arbitration and litigation.
- Understand the negotiation process and demonstrate the role of negotiator.
- Understand the mediation process and demonstrate the role of mediator.
- Empower others to resolve their conflicts.

Skill: Work Well in a Group: Behaviors

Level 1: Name and define positive and negative behaviors and group stages and roles.

- Name five or more positive group behaviors.
- Define behaviors given the name.
- Define the stages of groups.
- Define typical group member roles.

Level 2: Recognize group behaviors in oneself and others.

- After watching an interaction (live or on video) give specific instances and data to illustrate behaviors, stages and roles.
- After participating in group work, accurately identify one's own and others' specific behaviors and roles.

Level 3: Purposefully choose to practice positive behaviors.

- Observe a group interaction, analyze the situation and determine behaviors that would improve the group's effectiveness or relationships.
- While participating in a group, determine the productivity of the group, identify appropriate behaviors, and choose to practice those behaviors effectively.

Teaching the Skills

Professors and staff now have a level of detail that enables them to develop creative activities and assignments that directly focus on a behavior necessary to master a skill. At this point in the workshop, participants were given personal time to consider on which particular skill they wanted to focus their attention. With a few activities to generate creativity and energy to get them started, they were sent out to think about teaching. Ideas for the examples developed by the directors follow.

Skill: Managing Conflict

Skill Level 4: Behavior: Understand the mediation process and demonstrate the role of mediator.

Teaching Strategies:
- Readings
- Outline of a mediation process
- Observe a scripted mediation role play
- Participate as a mediator in a role play.

Skill: Work Well in a Group

Skill Level 2: Behavior: After watching an interaction (live or on video) give specific instances and data to illustrate behaviors, stages and roles.

Teaching Strategies:
- Videotape a group discussion among class members.
- Observe a small-group discussion of class members.
- Participate in a small-group discussion observed by external assessors.
- Participate in a virtual world problem-solving activity.

For teachers, this is by far the most exciting work. Generating creative ideas with role plays, projects, laboratories, readings and discussion groups energized all of the participants.

Assessing Leadership Skills

Many accrediting agencies, including the North Central Association of Colleges and Schools, are requiring colleges to demonstrate how they determine if they are accomplishing their goals—whether they are doing the right things and whether the things that they are doing have positive results. Of course, faculty members have always assessed students' knowledge through tests, but for many faculty and staff assessing these behavioral skills presents a new challenge. A key question that needs to be answered is "Why am I assessing this?" Reasons might include: to improve my ability to teach it, to evaluate student performance for a grade, to give student feedback that will help improve skills. Any single assessment could serve one or all of these purposes, but it is important to note that not all assessments need to serve all purposes. This was reassuring to the faculty, since "grading" people on skills such as integrity may be harder than assessing to provide feedback.

    Another important question to ask in assessing these skills is "Who can do the assessing?" If faculty assume all responsibility for assessment, it can create a large increase in their workload. However, depending on the purpose of the assessment, faculty can call on the students themselves to do self-assessment, on their peers, and on other members of the campus or local community. When assessing for growth rather than for a grade, a new world of possibilities opens.

Finally, there were concerns that even though a student might seem very responsible and accountable in a given class or exercise, he or she might that very evening engage in conduct that is irresponsible. It is important to remember that even when a professor assesses knowledge attainment, he or she cannot guarantee that a student will forever have this knowledge. Similarly, assessment of leadership and professional skills is based on one instance or one semester's worth of demonstrated ability, and the professor is not accountable beyond that.

The directors again provided examples of assessments for the skills presented earlier and encouraged participants to share ideas and work collaboratively to develop innovative ways to assess what they had decided to teach. The directors' examples follow.

Skill: Managing Conflict

Skill Level 4: Behavior: Understand the mediation process and demonstrate the role of mediator

Teaching Strategy: Participate as a mediator in a role play.

Assessment Strategies:

- Give out specific mediation evaluation forms in advance of the role play, listing expected behaviors.
- Observe and take notes on behavior.
- Have students observe the videotaped role play and answer reflection questions.
- Have a feedback conversation with each panel.

Skill: Work Well in a Group

Skill Level 2: Behavior: After watching an interaction (live or on video) give specific instances and data to illustrate behaviors, stages and roles.

Teaching Strategy: Participate in a small-group discussion of class members observed by external assessors.

Assessment Strategies:

- Have students rate themsevles on specific group behaviors.
- Have peers rate students on group behaviors.
- Have trained external assessors rate students on behaviors.
- Have external assessors meet with individual students to compare assessments.

(This exercise is based on a model used extensively at Alverno College.)

Once these assessments are conducted, professors can then study the results to determine the success of their strategies and the individual growth of students. To assist in planning and managing the information, the directors recommended the following chart and asked that participants use this chart in planning their individual projects.

Class: _____
Skill: _____

What general outcome are you seeking? (List a level of a skill.)	How will you know it if you see it? (List a behavior for that level.)	How will you help students learn it? (teaching strategies)	How can you measure the desired behavior? (assessment strategies)	What are the assessment findings?	What improvements might you make?

At the conclusion of the workshop, participants were asked to identify the leadership and professional goals that could be integrated in their student learning plans and also, in the upcoming semester, to include at least one skill in their classes and complete the chart above for that skill.

Results

To assess the success of this project as a whole, the opinions of the participants and the awareness and knowledge of the students were key indicators of success. At the end of the semester when they participated, professors and student affairs professors were asked several qualitative questions about their experience. The most telling responses were those to the question, "What is the most important thing you learned in this project?" A sampling of responses follows.

- How to better assess the amount of learning that has taken place among students.
- The GRID showing us how to conceptualize and operationalize; helps crystallize different ideas.
- Changing our culture of higher education at Franklin College is contingent on persons (like myself) being invited and prodded to change, as well as reinforced frequently later.

- Student growth is as important as student grades.
- This may be as complicated as I thought! May be manageable, however.
- A reconfirmed sense of how many groups in the college are operating on the basis of a very similar vision.
- Definitions of a variety of leadership skills. Ideas for how to implement in courses.
- I learned some good steps on how to plan and learn from assessment and how to implement professional/leadership goals into our classes/activities.
- Value of and need for interdepartmental discussion of teaching and assessing leadership goals as well as possible/different ways of their implementation.

A simple two-page survey was distributed to 263 students in 21 classes that professors had targeted to integrate at least one of the leadership and professional goals. Dr. Tim Garner, associate dean and institutional researcher, analyzed these surveys. The classes spanned the range of 100-, 200-, 300-, and 400- level departmental courses as well as general education courses. Students were asked to identify which skills were being taught in the course and to define these skills; 77.45 percent clearly articulated an acceptable definition. Students were then asked to describe a strategy or activity that had been used in the course to teach the skill and 96.05 percent could accurately identify how the skill was taught.

Finally, on a scale of 1 (strongly disagree) to 4 (strongly agree) students were asked to respond to two statements: "My understanding of this skill has been significantly enhanced as a result of my involvement in this course." Average responses ranged from a low of 2.69 to a high of 3.67. "I am now better prepared to use this skill outside the classroom as a result of my involvement in this course." Responses ranged from a low of 2.92 to a high of 3.57.

Conclusion

Once in a class discussion about charismatic leadership, a student asked if doing such a detailed analysis would take the magic out of a subject, which by its very nature defied an analytic study. A similar question might be raised here. Can one break down leadership into discrete measurable behaviors, which are developmentally defined and assessed? The authors of this paper do not believe that all the facets of leadership can be captured in the format offered here. When a biologist pins down a butterfly and studies its anatomy, the magic and beauty of its flight is lost. Nonetheless, valuable things are learned. Similarly, learning and practicing the behaviors and goals described in this paper contribute to one's mastery of leadership. Yet the magic of leadership comes in the moment when the leader draws on knowledge and experience to choose the right response to a dynamic situation.

This approach is not the only answer, but it is one way to help faculty, student affairs staff and work/study supervisors actually implement the teaching and assessing of leadership and professional skills.

BONNIE PRIBUSH is a professor of mathematical sciences and director of the Franklin College Leadership Program. Although her advanced degrees are in mathematics and computer science, in 1991 she co-authored a Lilly Endowment grant that created the Franklin College Leadership Program, and she has been its director ever since. She also developed and continues to direct the Leadership Johnson County program.

MARILYN BEDFORD was the director of professional development at Franklin College during the process outlined in this article. She is currently the community relations director with the Julian Center, an agency providing counseling, shelter and education for women and children who are survivors of domestic violence and abuse.

Functional Leadership: A Model for the 21st Century

By Elisabeth Cox and Cynthia House

EVERY LIVING THING IS DYNAMIC. NOTHING IS STATIC, AT LEAST not for long. The life and health of any living organism is dependent on its ability to change and adapt to the ecosystem in which it must live. To slow or limit this adaptation is to invite disease, ill health and premature aging. To arrest this adaptation is essentially choosing to die. Whether death is quick or slow, harsh or gracious, it is inevitable. As organization development practitioners, change agents, or leadership practitioners, we understand and even preach this truth. We intellectually and perhaps even spiritually understand the need for change and we advocate for it at every turn. Psychologically and particularly emotionally, however, we frequently resist making change in our own ways with equal, if not more, passion than we have advocated for it in the lives of others.

In most instances, we find it easier to direct others to change and to assist them in doing so than we find it easy to direct and assist ourselves. If we could be objective observers of our own behaviors, we might even view ourselves as hindrances to organizational, group, or community adaptation and change. If we were able to be self-reflective, we might even see ourselves as drawn to change agent roles because we are seeking ways to make change in our own lives more comfortable.

Perhaps the greatest paradox of life is that the very adaptation on which we depend to sustain us and the organizations, institutions and communities which we establish is the very requirement from which we desire the most freedom and over which we have the least control. As those practicing leadership, serving as change agents, and blazing new trails in organizational life and practice, we must be a source of renewal, an example of continual adaptation and change rather than a source of arrested development and resistance.

Becoming this source of renewal will require that we change our perspectives, that we give up established paradigms and methods of practice and move out of our comfort zone. We must ask ourselves hard questions. Do we behave as we do in our organizations, communities, and governments because we believe that doing so is in the best interest of the whole? Or do we behave as we do because it enables us to maintain some control, retain our expert status, and significantly reduce the anxiety and perhaps even the embarrassment that we feel when we do not have all the answers and cannot predict the future?

We believe that organizations are living organisms, at one with their members. And for organizations, as for all organisms, adaptation is the key to life and health. As change agents and as members, we must hold this truth sacred. What works today may not work tomorrow and what does not work today may very well work tomorrow.

It is with this spirit of openness to renewal and learning that we share with you our journey in the belief that this sharing and the resulting interactions and conversations will create new horizons and possibilities for us all.

The Journey

When we at Lazarus began our careers as organization development practitioners, we came to the work having had several years of experience in other careers. Because of this time spent as traditional members of the workforce, we understood that some things about how organizations were often structured and about how work and organizational life were often conducted were very dysfunctional and created tension for both the organization and its members. We were determined to make a difference in the lives of the organizations with whom we worked and in the lives of the members who composed these organizations by partnering with them to bring about change.

Our journey together as practitioners has been more emergent than planned, and we have always considered our work as much art as it is science. We have learned through our work with organizations or groups that if we can quiet the noise of "what has always been" in each situation we can hear the voice of "what will work best," what is logical and natural. In this respect, our experience tracks well with the principles of "the logic of life"[1] as theorized by Meg Wheatley and presented in her book *A Simpler Way:*

1. Everything is in a constant process of discovering and creating.
2. Life uses messes to get well-ordered solutions.
3. Life is intent on finding what works, not what's "right."
4. Life creates more possibilities as it engages with opportunities.

5. Life is attracted to order.

6. Life organizes around identity.

7 Everything participates in the creation and evolution of its neighbor.[2]

Our experiences have led us to these core beliefs about organizations and the people who define and give them life:

1. Everything is dynamic, constantly changing.
2. Ways of doing things that holistically work take precedence over tradition.
3. Finding ways that work means both destruction and creation.
4. Change in one area of a system impacts things in all other areas of the system.
5. Every person and thing is in relationship with every other person and thing in its environment.
6. Healthy relationships result in growth, adaptation and creation.
7. Unhealthy relationships result in stagnation, rigidity and destruction.

Our journey has been somewhat about finding ways to make these principles known, understood and applied in the organizational world. This has meant getting out of the box and thinking about organization development, organizations, and the people who give them life in really different and unique ways. We did not start out of the box, however. We started with the accepted models and methodologies of the time. However, regardless of whether we used these accepted models in their original form, in a somewhat altered form, or in some combined form, we found them of limited usefulness in bringing about the changes we were seeking.

For the sake of time and discussion, we have broken our journey into segments based on the methodology we used and the lessons we learned from its application that spurred us on to the next phase. We are certain that our journey is not at an end with our current understandings. Based on our own core beliefs, organizations will always be changing, and we will always be searching for something that works.

Increasing Tension in Organizations

During the 1980s and 1990s, the tension between organizations and their members increased at a fevered pitch. This fact was particularly true in service and knowledge-work organizations where members were well-educated, independent thinkers who wanted freedom to work and to give input. The closer we moved to the new millennium, the more the tension grew. Because most of our clients were service and knowledge-work organizations, we found ourselves trying to discover the roots of the tension. Our experience and assessments seemed to indicate that these tensions were greatest when a significant difference existed between work reality and home or personal reality.

Some of the issues we found were:

- The potential of members was often limited rather than enhanced.
- The creativity of members was not encouraged and often not welcomed.
- Reporting structure was often more important than intelligent work structures.
- Social realities of independence, equality, and group decision making were at odds with work realities of dependence, inequality, and chain-of-command decision making.
- Spirituality was missing from the work environment.
- Work lacked challenge and was not always fulfilling.
- Members were often given directives by those less knowledgeable, experienced or creative.
- Members' views of needed changes were largely ignored.
- Organizations did not easily adapt to changes in the environment.
- Equating growth in the organization with moving up the hierarchy limited the potential for growth and focused the attention on politics rather than on professional and personal development.

We realize now that the tensions we were experiencing were very much related to the fading Industrial Economy and the emerging Creative Economy. We also understand that our quest to help create an organization that was more socially informed was very much related to the emerging Creative Economy.

Phase 1: Altering the "How" and Assuming the "What"

As new consultants, we followed what was then a fairly common practice; we helped our client organizations change how things were done and didn't spend a great deal of time questioning whether or not the things themselves were appropriate. It wasn't the management structure that was the problem, for example; it was how we practiced management. It wasn't the work structure that was the problem; it was lack of a quality program. It wasn't the work that teams were given to do, their role in the organization, or their degree of autonomy or authority; it was how they held meetings, brainstormed around problems, and shared space.

Some of our realizations during this phase were:

- Emphasis was on improving the "how" of work.
- In most organizations, the message was that the "what" was OK and

untouchable.

- This fact was further driven home because formal leaders usually decided the "whats."
- Business logic was the order of the day and was more important than human logic, spirituality, intuition or social awareness.
- Organizations and membership were not viewed as the same, and not only were they different, they were viewed as vastly unequal in importance.
- Leadership was primarily performed by a person in a position.

Though we quickly became disillusioned with these narrowly defined projects, we did extensive work in this area. We have noted below some of our typical work from our earlier practice:

- participative management development
- participative supervisory training
- participative decision-making training
- quality improvement and total quality management implementation
- team development using a four-phase model with teams whose members had less than full-time involvement
- team assessments based on simulations rather than on genuine involvement
- enriching jobs
- strategic planning done by the executive group
- business planning done by the managers
- custom training programs designed to meet needs determined by management.

However, within a short time, we discovered that just altering "how" things were done was not enough. Though our client organizations usually enjoyed improved performance and members were more satisfied with their work and organizational life, the improvements were not enough in the long term. Tensions were just increasing. We were not facilitating the transformational changes necessary to address the complex cultural and ecological problems we believed were eroding the effectiveness of organizations of all kinds and demoralizing their members.

Phase 2: Reconfiguring the "What" and Altering the "How"

We would like to report that at this point we repented of our ignorance, changed directions, and lived happily ever after. In actuality, we did repent of our ignorance, and we did change direction. We did not, however, live happily ever after. We began experimenting, changing "what" was being done as well as "how" things were being done in the hope of having a more significant impact on the complex ills we saw engulfing the organizations with whom we worked.

Some of our realizations during this phase were:

- Organizational ills and problems are very complex and don't lend themselves to quick or simple fixes.
- Just giving members the skills to do things better will not solve all the problems.
- Assessments are a necessity and the best way to gather objective information about all aspects of the organization.
- Formal leaders tend to own any change process and usually attempt to control it.
- Change is both feared and resisted by most members, even those who believe it necessary.

Reconfiguring the "what" involved us in such efforts as:

- implementing fully autonomous teams within an organization
- flattening the hierarchy and eliminating management layers
- implementing cross-functional teams with complete authority to perform
- implementing a horizontal work structure
- developing a seven phase model for team development.

Though we were still seeing improvements in performance and morale in the organizations and the work was much more challenging and interesting to us, we still were not getting the measure of impact we desired. The tensions were still rising.

Phase 3: Putting New Wine in Old Wineskins

We realized that the more socially informed ideas and practices about work had to find their way into the knowledge and service-work organizations with whom we worked. Our next direction was to take the concepts of "workplace communities" and to try to implement them in our client organizations. Since most organizations were maintaining the traditional, hierarchical framework, we had to lay these "soft skills" over the traditional organization structure. The results were still significantly less than we had hoped for. While members of the organization responded well to the concepts and learned new ways of interacting, communicating and dealing with problems, they were not always able to practice what they were learning. The organizations in structure and practice were still very traditional and hierarchical, leaving little room for the more open, community-based communication and interactions.

Some of our realizations during this phase were:

- People and organizations are one.
- Socially informed philosophies about work had been virtually ignored and had to be inserted in the mix.
- Social philosophies about work can be laid over the traditional organization with only limited success.
- Members had to learn self-awareness, relationship skills, group skills—the hard "soft" skills.
- Members were not able to practice their new skills because the traditional environment was still alive and well.

We did such work projects as:

- charting points of integration and designing integration processes
- facilitating negotiations involving professional feedback issues
- shifting the organization from a department focus to a work team focus
- designing horizontal work structures
- designing conflict management processes.

Phase 4: Creating and Innovation—A Better Track

Because of our experiences with workplace communities, we knew that something more drastic would have to be implemented to overcome and/or change the culture of any organization. We had, for all practical purposes, given up on finding an existing model that would enable us to realize our goal. Since a portion of what was going wrong with our client organizations could be traced to the formal and even informal leaders, we decided that it was time to give up on existing models and create some totally new ways of thinking about and practicing leadership. We began to question the validity of what had always been considered good business practice.

It was during this time as well, that we also came to understand the extent of the tension in many organizations and arrived at some wisdom about the causes. The industrial economy was dying; the creative economy was emerging and all bets were off. The foundation of the creative economy is based on the sale of ideas and concepts and the services that come from these. Organizational practices had to change to meet the challenges of the 21st century.

We are still at this point in our journey. We are learning, innovating and sharing more than we ever imagined possible.

Some of our realizations during this phase have been:

- Creativity and innovation are central to the new economy.

- The self and the self in relationship to other people and other things are the core of every organization.
- Healthy relationships engender creativity.
- Leadership is a set of functions that must be done by everyone.
- Management is a set of functions that must be done by everyone.

Out of this effort came the framework for what we dubbed the "Collaborative Organization" and "Functional Leadership." The collaborative structure differs from other organizational structures in that the power is equally distributed throughout the organization and the work is maintained and changed by dialogue, interaction and negotiation. Functional Leadership was unique in that it approached leadership as a set of things that had to be done, not as a position or a personality that had to be acquired.

This functional approach to leadership meant that all members of the organization could learn to practice leadership and would be accountable for doing so. At this point, we really felt that we had reached Mecca. However, our excitement was short lived because those practicing functional leadership and collaboration were still running into barriers in the organization. To end our frustration, we decided to really examine the traditions of organizations and to identify those that hindered the full implementation of Functional Leadership or collaborative work structures.

What we discovered was that we had backed into the place where we likely should have started our work several years before. What we needed was an entirely new model for business. We needed a model that was consistent with what was important to those in the workforce, that would enable organizations to move into and take advantage of the coming economy, and that was conducive to rapid adaptation and change. We arrived at the *Relational Model for Business.*

The Relational Organization Model

For more than eighty years now business has followed the mechanistic[3] model and lived out the belief that the purpose of business is to create and control wealth. As this model has worked less and less well, we have modified it, applied management and motivation theories to it, and tried every structure from hierarchy to teams to keep the model effective. However, even with all our efforts, very few of us have ever stopped to seriously consider the current validity of the model itself or the core belief on which it was built.

However, we found that challenging the model and its core belief was not only appropriate, it was mandatory if we were ever to experience more socially informed organizations. Any model that treats people as machines and primarily a means to an end is no longer relevant or a good fit for today's businesses.

We challenge the assumption that people are machines, expendable cogs replaceable on a whim, or resources waiting to be used. We do believe that financial reward is ultimately a result of business. However, we seriously question that it is the *purpose* of business.

The principles of scientific management and the methods employed by Frederick Taylor during the Industrial Era will not be able to affect the kind of widespread, radical change needed to align business with who we are as humans or with the creative economy, which has already been birthed.

For us, the purpose of business is to provide a venue for healthy and productive relationships out of which the creation of new goods, services, information or knowledge is possible. Creativity happens the most effectively in the context of people and things in their environment working together well and the least effectively in the context of people and things in their environment working together poorly. Business is about relationships, and not just those with other organization members. It is people in relationship with clients and customers, with vendors, with technology, with the market and the industry, with the organization culture, with work process, and with systems.

> **FOR US, THE PURPOSE OF BUSINESS IS TO PROVIDE A VENUE FOR HEALTHY AND PRODUCTIVE RELATIONSHIPS OUT OF WHICH THE CREATION OF NEW GOODS, SERVICES, INFORMATION OR KNOWLEDGE IS POSSIBLE.**

Business is about relationships that foster creativity. Creation tends to result in financial returns. However, creation rarely happens from focusing on finances. To make the leap back to its beginning, business must have at its heart the essence of what it means to be human—which we don't think is about creating or generating money, though that is a necessity of living. Instead, it is more about creating meaning, ending each day, each month, each year, and ultimately a lifetime feeling a sense of fulfillment at what we have done with our time. For most of us, meaning comes from relationships and from what we ultimately contribute to our world however we define it.

Business must begin to see itself as a vehicle through which we can create meaning in our lives, and to understand that the better the vehicle the more meaning we can create. The more meaning we can create, the more innovations in products, services and knowledge we can produce. The more innovations we produce, the more likely we are to adapt and remain successful over time in all ways, including financially.

Our questioning has led us to the belief that every member of the organization must attend to seven critical business needs if the organization is to become a healthy, ecological business community—stable, productive and adaptable. Ownership of these critical needs means that members must apply themselves to and are responsible for performing membership functions, management functions and leadership functions in each of the seven critical areas.

Functional Leadership: A New Philosophy

The conceptualization of leadership that we have come to is function centered rather than person centered. This conceptualization is a departure from the traditional thinking about leadership, which focuses more on the person practicing the leadership than on the things being practiced. This traditional view holds as its central tenant that an individual must have or develop certain personal characteristics to effectively practice leadership or to be an effective leader. The traditional understanding essentially means that good leadership is only possible for those who are born with or who have developed certain personal characteristics or who have learned a certain way of being in the world.

Much research has been conducted on leadership using this traditional person-centered view. A digest of the bulk of this research seems to indicate that someone who is able to be an effective leader is ambitious, achievement oriented, energetic and tenacious. In addition, he or she has integrity and is honest, self-confident, emotionally stable, creative, flexible, charismatic, dominant, conscientious, open to change. He or she possesses technical knowledge, has superlative people and management skills, and has the ability to think and reason intelligently, develop and articulate a vision, take risks, build teams and manage information. Finally, he or she must be able to motivate others, effectively hire and train staff members, and structure work.

In short, the people able to be strong leaders are quite extraordinary and, in our estimation, few and far between. In reality, it is not possible for any one person to be equally gifted in all the ways mentioned above. This means that when only a few are empowered to practice leadership, some things will be attended to very well; other things will be attended to less well, and still other things will not be attended to at all.

Function-centered leadership is the practice of leadership as a set of things that must be done to take care of the organization's critical needs rather than as a set of characteristics that must be acquired in order to be a leader. Since these critical business needs are expressed throughout the organization day in and day out, in strategic and operational ways, both formally and informally, we believe they cannot be well-attended if only those in positions of formal authority are chartered with their care. If everyone is practicing leadership, however, all the needs of the organization are much more likely to be met and in more effective ways.

Functional leadership can and should be practiced by everyone in the organization at any point that a need arises. When everyone is practicing leadership, no one person has to be gifted in all functions. Certain members will usually have a natural ability or giftedness in certain leadership functions. However, it is rare to see any one member with natural giftedness in all seven functions. Each person can operate in his or her strongest gifts and all the needs of the organization will be attended in the best ways possible.

Although Functional Leadership principles can be applied to a traditional power structure, we believe that for an organization to be fully healthy, to be fully stable, productive and adaptable, every member must practice leadership. At Lazarus, we are now in the business of teaching the practice of leadership to all members of our client organizations.

The Seven Leadership Functions

Functional Leadership as conceptualized and developed by Lazarus consists of seven functions or sets of things that must be done. These functions are broad categories of activities that are used to respond to the seven critical business needs of the organization.

Assessing

One of the most important leadership functions is assessment. Continuously assessing the organization and its ecology is critical to the continued life and health of the organization. Assessment is the precursor to any formal or informal change within the organization.

Assessing involves:

1. Scanning organizational ecology.
2. Questioning Status Quo.
3. Determining needed sources of data
4. Gathering global and specific data.

5. Synthesizing information.

6. Hypothesizing possibilities.

7. Recommending changes, new directions, and new ways of doing things.

This task of assessment requires objectivity, clarity and the ability to synthesize lots of information from many different sources so that we will know when, where and how to make changes.

Internal Aligning

Equally important to protecting the culture and attending to the continued health of the organization is the leadership function of Internal Alignment. Aligning internally means that we understand what is important to the organization and its members and know where it is headed to then be able to ensure that all activities and decisions are consist with this data.

Internal Alignment involves the following:

1. Championing organizational values.

2. Devising strategies consistent with organizational values.

3. Aligning work structure with organizational values.

4. Aligning processes with organizational values.

5. Aligning systems with organizational values.

6. Making decisions consistent with organizational values.

7. Practicing behaviors consistent with organizational values.

Once the vision and values of the organization have been determined and everyone understands and shares a belief in what is important, then these values must be lived out in the daily operations of the organization. The alignment function allows the organization to actually practice what it preaches by keeping the culture and business practices of the organization aligned with its vision and values. When inconsistencies arise, those practicing leadership must hold firm to the vision and values of the organization.

Altering

A major function of leadership is determining needed changes. In order to stay healthy and meet the demands being placed on the organization, it must be in constant change. Those practicing leadership must be the agents for this constant adaptation.

Being an effective change agent involves:

1. Planning for needed changes.

2. Examining execution of the plan.

3. Questioning viability of the plan.

4. Making needed adjustments.

5. Evaluating results with an objective eye.

6. Synchronizing global implementation of the plan.

7. Evaluating ongoing global impact of the plan.

Once the organization, the environment, the systems, the processes and the integration of all of these within the organization or any problems or opportunities that may present themselves have been assessed, we must plan for the needed changes. Once these plans are made, they must be implemented and the implementation monitored so that needed adjustments to the plans can be made.

Initiating

One of the demands or most important requirements of those practicing leadership is to initiate totally new things into the organization, the unit or the team. These new things can be new members, new teams, new projects, new processes, new systems, new ways of solving problems, new ways of planning, or even new ways of celebrating.

Initiating involves:

1. Visioning possibilities for the future.

2. Innovating to realize the vision.

3. Designing new processes and systems.

4. Starting new operational activities.

5. Locating necessary resources for initiatives.

6. Providing support and involvement with initiatives.

7. Evaluating progress of initiatives.

New times and new demands require new strategies. Sometimes just tweaking the old ways or just having the same members will not meet the demands of the environment or our own demands for challenge and growth. As members practicing leadership, we must be sensitive to the need for a new way and initiate new orders. However, whatever is initiated, part of the initiation function is to secure whatever resources are needed for the effort to be successful, including coaching and support, and monitoring during the initiation period.

Facilitating

Facilitation means influencing the interaction of others so that the most effective and efficient performance of the tasks at hand can be realized.

Facilitation involves:

1. Influencing free flow of leadership, management, membership and business information.
2. Influencing caring interactions.
3. Influencing courageous behaviors.
4. Requiring consensus decisions.
5. Influencing personal ownership.
6. Influencing alignment and integration of all activities.
7. Encouraging personal and professional growth.

Practicing leadership facilitation means influencing the flow of membership, leadership, and task information so that all the data is being presented. Good decisions cannot be made unless all the needed information is on the table. Facilitating may mean guiding interactions during a meeting, encouraging discussions on difficult issues and conflict management so that relationships are not damaged. Facilitation may require that we encourage courageous behavior when information is being withheld or that we work for true consensus on difficult decisions.

Leadership facilitates the smooth interaction of people, processes, and systems. Facilitation is the guiding touch, the grease that allows everything to flow smoothly. This does not mean that facilitation enables things to run smoothly for the short term. Sometimes practicing good facilitation means asking hard questions or making members uncomfortable.

Integrating

Another function of leadership is integration. Integration means that people, processes, and systems within the team, the unit and across the organization connect, fit well together and are improved or changed as needed.

Practicing integration involves:

1. Determining points of internal integration.
2. Determining points of external integration.
3. Connecting with everyone involved.
4. Establishing integration processes.
5. Evaluating integration processes.
6. Allocating necessary resources.
7. Synchronizing global integration.

Integration is perhaps the most overlooked and undervalued function of leadership. It is, however, one of the main reasons why systems, processes, projects and collaborations of all kinds are successful or unsuccessful. Well-defined and designed points of integration will result in efficient and effective operations across the organization. Integration can be thought of as the operational grease, just as facilitation is the interaction grease. Smooth integration makes everyone feel good about the work being accomplished.

Educating
Practicing leadership also involves providing others with the education they will need to perform well in the organization and its environment.

Educating involves:

1. Ascertaining needed knowledge, skills, and abilities.
2. Ascertaining individual giftedness and preferences.
3. Teaching to impact knowledge.
4. Training to provide skills.
5. Providing opportunities for experience.
6. Coaching to increase abilities.
7. Guiding to recognize wisdom gained.

Determining what knowledge, skills or abilities are needed is the first step in practicing the leadership function of education. This determination can be made formally through testing or evaluations or informally through observation or discussion.

How these functions are attended to and by whom will vary from organization to organization. If any organization is to be productive, stable and adaptable, leadership must practiced. Simply giving someone or some group the title of leader is no guarantee that leadership will happen. Leadership is a set of things that must be done in a specified way and by specified people—whether this is a few people in formal positions or everyone in the organization.

A Few Key Learnings of Our Journey Thus Far:

- Each organization is unique.
- Cookie-cutter approach doesn't work because of the variation among organizations.
- Not all members are happy about being given authority to make decisions.
- Not all members want to be responsible for the life and health of the business.
- Not all executives and managers are resistant to giving away or sharing authority with members.
- Not all members are excited about working on a team.
- Not all members are willing or able to be self-reflective.

- Without self-awareness, healthy relationships are difficult.
- Personal courage is important in a relational organization.
- Formal leaders do not always know what is best for the organization.
- Change takes time—almost always more time than you think it will.

We hope you have enjoyed this glimpse of our journey as organization development practitioners and that you have benefited from and perhaps related to some of the things we have learned along the way. We also hope you will ponder Functional Leadership and perhaps try it on for size. We think you will find it meaningful.

ELISABETH COX has an MBA from the University of Tennessee, Knoxville, and is currently an organization development practitioner with Lazarus Consulting Group, Inc., based in Knoxville, TN. Elisabeth has over ten years of experience as a researcher and practitioner in the organization development field. She has also worked with an international consulting firm, with the University of Tennessee's Management Development Center, and TVA's Corporate Human Resource Center.

CYNTHIA HOUSE has an MA in Liberal Arts from Murray State University in western Kentucky and is currently an organization development practitioner with Lazarus Consulting Group, Inc, based in Knoxville, TN. Cynthia has fifteen years of experience as a theorist and practitioner in the organization development field. Previously, she was vice-president of training and curriculum design for a national training firm and was a college instructor for seven years.

[1] Wheatley, M. (1996). *A Simpler Way*, p. 13

[2] Ibid, p. 14.

[3] The mechanistic or scientific model on which business has operated since the Industrial Age of Henry Ford and Frederick Taylor is based on Newton's laws of nature. From the 1680s onward, Newton measured things that were fairly predictable in movement and objects that could be seen or felt. From his observations he developed a few simple equations for measuring input and output. Newton's laws seemed to have such universal application, they became the organizing principle of business—output is equal to input. The machine became the mental model for thinking about and organizing people. Taylor later argued that "all possible brain work should be removed from the shop" and jobs, like machines, became ever more specialized and repetitive.

Political Leadership in An Age of Cynicism

By Michael A. Genovese

TO EVERYTHING THERE IS A SEASON. JUST AS THE SEASONS OF THE year change, so too do the seasons of leadership and politics change. Leadership is almost wholly contextual. There is no one leadership style for all seasons. Different conditions, different demands, different constitutional/structural designs, different personalities, all change the shape of the leadership style required to meet the demands of the situation.

In effect, the music changes, and the leader needs to adapt and adjust, fitting the dance to the music being played. Rarely can the leader change the music him or herself. Often, leadership is a response (sometimes functional, sometimes dysfunctional) to the conditions imposed from without.

Leaders do not lead in a vacuum. There is a context, and that context changes. In normal times, the United States system (separation of powers, checks and balances) imposes a near straitjacket restriction on presidential leadership. However, during a crisis, the checks and balances usually give way to wider latitude in which presidents can more freely act.

The Age of Cynicism

Today we live in what should be called an *Age of Cynicism*. Beginning with Vietnam and Watergate, this cynicism has all but consumed our political landscape. In a post Viet-gate era, the public has become more cynical and apathetic, the press more intrusive and investigative, the parties more divisive and attack-oriented. The pursuit of scandal has replaced competition over philosophical differences, and a form of political cannibalism has replaced normal discourse and competition. "Ethics investigations" are now an accepted form of politics as usual.[1]

These deep partisan scars were most visible during the failed efforts by Republicans to remove President Clinton from office in 1998-1999 via impeachment and conviction. But the trench warfare of '98-99 has roots in the politics and culture wars of the 1960s. The "scorched earth" policy made infamous by Newt

Gingrich has now become the norm in political life. Is it any wonder that citizens are cynical?

Such an age has consequences for leadership, followership and citizenship. The chief characteristics of this age of cynicism are:

- low trust in government
- low voter turnout
- high anti-incumbent feelings
- the rise of non-traditional candidates
- highly volatile voting patterns
- a warping of civic engagement
- growth of meanness and incivility (e.g., road rage)
- the emergence of "slash-and-burn" politics
- hyper-partisanship
- the personalization of political opposition
- the criminalization of policy differences
- the rise of the "angry white male" voter.

Why, after a series of what most objective observers would characterize as successes, are citizens of the United States so cynical?[2] After all, in the past sixty years, the United States was largely responsible for defeating Marxism and Communism, building a free-trade/democracy regime of global proportions, building an economy that is robust and the envy of the world, building the world's strongest military machine, expanding civil rights for its citizens, starting to bring women and minorities toward achieving equality in a world where no nation poses a great threat to our national security, and even crime is down!

If we are so successful, why do we feel beaten and defeated? Put another way, if we are so rich, why do we feel so poor? The better things seem to get, the worse we seem to feel.

Journalist E.J. Dionne, noting the decline of civility in politics, wrote that the legacy of the past 30 years is a "polarized politics that highlights symbolic issues, short-circuits genuine political debate, ...and leaves the country alarmed."[3]

A 1996 study by the Center for National Policy entitled "Diagnosing Voter Discontent" reported that, "The American political system has been experiencing a level of cynicism and public dissatisfaction that is unusual by historic standards."[4] This discontent has consequences. Many Americans have, in an effort to assign blame, turned inward and pointed the guilty finger at "the government."

When did Americans start hating their government? "In truth," Michael Nelson writes, "there has never been a time when Americans were pro-politics and pro-politicians."[5] Americans early on developed a very individualistic, rights-based political culture, and as we have always had a love-hate relationship with government, we yearn for the fruits of government largesse, yet fear an intrusive or abusive state. Thomas Paine declared, "Government, even its best state, is but a necessary evil." But have we gone too far? Clearly the anti-government/anti-politics sentiments have consequences. As British journalist Gavin Esler observes:

> The crisis of American democracy means weak leaders with weak mandates lead weak political parties at a time of great social upheaval, but it extends far further. The federal government, constructed as the servant of the people, is now frequently reviled as an increasingly despotic or greedy master, or alternatively seen as utterly disconnected from the daily lives of most citizens…
>
> One result is that fear and hatred of Communism as the greatest threat to the American way of life has given way to fear and hatred of the U.S. federal government itself. Washington has replaced Moscow as the city Americans love to hate. The "red scare" of anti-Communism witch-hunts of the 1940s and 50s has become the "fed scare" of anti-government paranoia in the 1990s. The fed scare is most angrily exposed on the far right-wing fringes of anti-government militias and their supporters.[6]

It should be noted that distrust of government has a long and distinguished pedigree in the United States. This nation was founded by rebels who fought against governmental authority. Ours is a doubting people. We have a long, rich history of being anti-government and anti-politics.[7]

In fact, a little disrespect is a good thing. But disrespect can go too far. It can undermine self-government and weaken the bonds of community. Of course, one person's disrespect is another person's blow against tyranny. But lines can be drawn, distinctions made.

A strong democracy requires a healthy dose of skepticism. A democratic people is a doubting people. If the people are too complacent or trusting, they can more easily be led down the path to despotism. If, however, they display a healthy level of doubt, their burden of proof sharpens rather than diminishes the critical faculties of citizens, and a robust rather than a dormant democracy is possible.

But there is a fine line between skepticism and cynicism. A skeptical people always run the risk that in troubled times they will sink into despair and cynicism. A cynic is one who doubts the sincerity and legitimacy of nearly everything, or as H.L. Mencken noted, a cynic is "someone who, when he smells flowers wonders: where is the funeral?" Cynicism breeds distrust, disrespect and divisiveness. It lowers citizen and voter participation and undermines democratic vigor. Today, the United States has sunk into an Age of Cynicism.[8]

By almost any measure, the nation's skepticism has degenerated into a dangerous level of cynicism that threatens the very core of self-government today (see Tables 1 and 2).

TABLE 1: National Election Studies Measures of Trust and Efficacy, 1964-1992

Trust: How much of the time do you think you can trust the government in Washington to do what is right—just about always, most of the time, or only some of the time?

	1964	1968	1972	1976	1980	1984	1988	1992
Always	14%	8%	7%	3%	2%	4%	4%	3%
Most of the time	62	53	45	29	23	40	36	26
Some or none of the time	22	37	45	29	23	40	36	26
Don't Know/Not ascertained	2	2	3	1	2	2	2	2
Total	100%	100%	100%	100%	100%	100%	100%	100%

Source: National Election Studies, 1952-1992.

TABLE 2: Alienation and Distrust, 1952-1992

While government is but the most glaring target of the public's cynicism, citizen cynicism extends to a variety of other institutions as well (see Table 3). We have become a deeply cynical people.

	Alienation	Distrust
1952	20%	*
1956	16	*
1960	21	*
1964	21	22%
1968	35	37
1972	31	45
1976	36	62
1980	26	73
1984	26	54
1988	27	58
1992	30	69

*Question not asked prior to 1964.

Source: National Election Studies, 1952-1992.

TABLE 3: Confidence in American Institutions

Question: I am going to name some institutions in this country. As far as the people running these institutions are concerned, would you say you have a great deal of confidence, only some confidence, or hardly any confidence at all in them?

	1991	1993	1994	1996
Congress	18%	7%	8%	8%
Executive branch	26	12	11	10
Military	60	42	37	37
Banks & financial institutions	12	15	18	25
Major companies	20	21	25	23
Organized labor	11	8	10	11
The press	16	11	10	11
Television	14	12	10	10
Education	30	22	25	23
Organized religion	25	23	24	25
Medicine	47	39	42	45
Scientific community	40	38	38	39

Source: Public Perspective, February/March 1997, pp. 2-5.

The undermining of civic engagement in this age of cynicism has weakened the connection of citizens to each other and to the state, thereby depleting the "social capital" of political efficacy and participation. Civic participation in community groups has been declining, and a more personalized, individualistic citizen has emerged. "Politics by other means"[9] has slowly been replacing more conventional civic forms of practice.

As W. Lance Bennett points out, the fear of the post-World War II era, as reflected in the writings of Laswell and Fromin, that the individual was in jeopardy of losing identity to the group, in the 1990s, is that the collective identity may be so weak and the individual so strong (e.g., the rise of isolating technologies such as the personal computer) as to risk losing a group or community identity to the imperial self.[10]

The glue that connects individual to community binds but loosely in this age of cynicism. We become more disengaged from our fellow citizens and more critical of the state. Robert D. Putnam defined social capital as "features of social life—networks, norms, and trust—that enable participants to act together more effectively to pursue shared objectives."[11] In place of social capital, we have the rise of "the uncivic culture."[12]

And while the United States is not alone in this cynicism toward government, there are precious few nations whose citizens equal the U.S. distrust in government. As the data in Table 4 makes clear, the U.S. ranks ninth out of twelve countries on the trust in government scale. Only Italy, Belgium and France fall below the United States.

TABLE 4: Comparative Alienation: United States and Europe

Country	Trust government all or most of the time, percentages and rank
United States	34 (9)
West Germany	52 (5)
Netherlands	46 (7)
Austria	55 (4)
United Kingdom	40 (8)
Finland	50 (6)
Switzerland	76 (1)
Italy	14 (12)
Greece	62 (2)
Denmark	56 (3)
France	33 (10)
Belgium	20 (11)

Sources: Samuel H. Barnes and Max Kaase et al., "Political Action: An Eight-Nation Study, 1973-1976," Inter-University Consortium for Political and Social Research Codebook, cited in Raymond E. Wolfinger, David P. Glass, and Peverill Squire, "Predictors of Electoral Turnout: An International Comparison," Policy Studies Review 9 (Spring 1990): 557; Commission of the European Communities, Euro-Barometre, no. 17 (June 1982): 25; and 1980 National Election Study Codebook 1:614, variable 1030, cited in Wolfinger, Glass, and Squire, "Predictors of Electoral Turnout."

The Causes of Cynicism

What has caused this plunge into the depths of cynicism? While the reasons are many, two factors stand out as especially germane: seminal events and the crisis of modernization.

Events

In his 1961 inaugural address, President John F. Kennedy articulated an optimistic, expansive view of the American mission. We would, he asserted, "pay any price and bear any burden" to support freedom and democracy. Kennedy inspired a generation of Americans to get involved in politics. He spoke of public service as noble and good.

But Kennedy's call to action was the denouement of Americans' belief that the future was theirs. From that time on, events came crashing down on American optimism. First, a series of political assassinations devastated the national psyche — John Kennedy in 1963, Martin Luther King in 1968, and Robert F. Kennedy in 1968. Then came Vietnam, the war that the U.S. could not win and from which it could not honorably withdraw. The failure of America's Vietnam policy brought deep divisions at home. "The Sixties," that time of counter-cultural social upheaval, was a movement against authority and "the establishment." It undermined tradition and called authority (also known as leadership) into question.

Vietnam was followed almost immediately by Watergate,[13] and the single most corrupt presidential administration in U.S. history. Richard Nixon undermined public confidence in government at a time when public cynicism was already growing. A long, unpopular war was followed by scandal. The public reacted.[14]

> **" IT SHOULD BE NOTED THAT DISTRUST OF GOVERNMENT HAS A LONG AND DISTINGUISHED PEDIGREE IN THE UNITED STATES. "**

In response to Vietnam and Watergate, the public grew increasingly self-centered. By the 1980s, Ronald Reagan and a *Culture of Greed* swept the nation. Public-spiritedness declined. Self-interest increased. "Government," President Reagan often said, "is the problem." Indeed, it may have appeared that way to many. To make matters worse, during the Reagan years, the Iran-Contra scandal broke, further breaking the bond of trust of citizen to government.

In the 1990s, character and sex scandals of the Clinton presidency and the rise of the slash-and-burn politics of Newt Gingrich further increased public distaste for politics and politicians. All of these troubles occurred in the midst of economic plenty (for the top of the economic ladder at least).

Today, images of hate flood the airwaves. Television programs such as the popular "Jerry Springer Show" regularly show scenes of violence, conflict, and hatred—as entertainment. Talk radio is full of racist, hateful messages. The Internet has become a haven for hate-mongers.

What are the consequences of the deluge of hate messages? A pollster on National Public Radio reported recently that, "30 percent of the public wants Clinton killed."[15] Theologian Martin Marty quotes philosopher Eric Hoffer, who called hate "the most accessible and comprehensive of all unifying agents."[16] But as we know, most hatred is a form of projection. As the character in Hermann Hesse's *Demian* notes, "If you hate a person, you hate something in him that is part of yourself."

That so much of today's politics of hate comes from extremist religious fundamentalists is surprising to some, not so unexpected to others. William Hazlitt, in his 1825 essay, "On the Pleasure of Hating," wrote that "the pleasures of hating, like a poisonous mineral, eats into the heart of religion and turns it to rankling spleen and bigotry…it leaves to virtue nothing but the spirit of censoriousness." And as Jonathan Swift noted, "We have just enough religion to make us hate, but not enough to make us love one another." Martin Luther King, Jr., offered the following solution to the problem: "Hatred and bitterness can never cure the disease of fear; only love can do that. Hatred paralyzes life; love releases it. Hatred confuses life; love harmonizes it. Hatred darkens life; love illuminates it."[17]

Vietnam and Watergate spawned cynicism toward government — the government, as President Reagan reminded an already cynical public, was the enemy. Such cynicism led to a turning away from government as problem solver, and voters turned inward. The self was elevated, the commonweal desecrated. Public service, a noble endeavor in 1960, was viewed with contempt in the 1980s and '90s. All these events led to public disaffection, anti-incumbent attitudes, and overall cynicism.[18]

Modernization

We live in a world where the only constant is change, rapid change. In a fast-moving world, our security blanket is removed. We have no anchor, and confusion and anxiety rule. The old anchors and past certainties no longer supply meaning and security. It is a high-stress world where values and traditions are threatened, and our comfort zones are shattered.[19]

A high-flux world requires a high-flex response. But most of us are not capable—do not have the training or the psyches—for such quick adaptations. Change is the norm. Technology changes by the minute, we live in a more interdependent world, it's all so damn confusing!

In general, how do we cope with the stresses of modernization? There are four basic responses to these changes. First, we can adapt, no easy task these days. Second, we can retreat into fundamentalism, searching for the security of simple certainties and absolute truths. Third is the retro solution, returning to older tradition and rituals, trying to recapture meaning. Finally, we often respond with anger, we blame others for our problems (e.g., immigrants or minorities), we lash out (e.g., hate radio), we seek revenge.

Leadership in a Cynical Age

It is difficult to lead well even in the best of circumstances. In a cynical age it may seem an impossible task. Followership—always difficult to elicit—seems a hopeless goal. How does a leader rebuild the ties that over the past forty years have been severed? How do you persuade people to give, make sacrifices, pull together, when most either don't trust or are openly hostile to government? How do we rekindle the bonds of nationhood and community? Can a public official speak to higher values and appeal to the best in citizens?[20]

In part, the culture shapes options. But leaders are not completely helpless. In a democracy, we tend to get the government we deserve. Rarely do "leaders" truly lead. Usually they follow, are compelled to give the people what they want and demand. Most demands for change (and the political leadership that accompanies it) percolate up (except in foreign policy); they emerge from the times and the culture. John Kennedy may have acted boldly on civil rights, but only after it became "safe" to do so. Ronald Reagan wasn't exercising leadership when he ran in 1980 on a promise to cut taxes by a third—he was giving the people what they already wanted.

If most "leaders" don't lead, but follow, is there a role for true leadership in an age of cynicism? Our guide in an age of cynicism—and in any age—can be found by combining lessons on leadership from two Mt. Rushmore presidents, Jefferson and Lincoln, into a Model of Democratic Leadership. Jefferson argued the role of a leader in a democracy is to work to educate and persuade the people, but ultimately, follow their will. This can be a slow process, and there is no guarantee of success. If we add to Jefferson's call the words of Abraham Lincoln, who hoped to appeal to the "better angels within us," we have the essential ingredients of something called "democratic leadership"—educate, appeal to what is best in people, follow the will of the citizens.

Can one exercise a form of democratic leadership in an age of cynicism, or, in a cynical age, should a president merely reflect and exploit that cynicism? In California, former Governor Pete Wilson seemed to make a career of exploiting cynicism, be it immigrant bashing, bilingual bashing, or just plain bashing. It proved electorally successful, but was it politically wise? While sound public policy arguments can be made for both sides of these serious public policy issues, these arguments were only marginal to Governor Wilson's strategy. He exploited emotion, appealed to a raw nerve in people, used the issues not to enlighten or appeal to the better angels within us, but to bludgeon opponents. Wilson ended up winning elections, but the rancor and bitterness he caused made him only marginally effective as a governor and helped mobilize Hispanic voters who ended up voting for Wilson's Democratic opponents!

Just as the age of cynicism closes many doors to leadership, the irony may be that as some doors close, others open. In an age of confusion and cynicism, the president's role as Shaman-in-chief becomes potentially more important.[21] In some ways, the president plays an important symbolic, quasi-religious role. As our national shaman, a president can simplify a complex world, provide reassurance, clarify simple truths, appeal to what is best in citizens, articulate a positive vision, provide direction and meaning, offer hope and security, give the appearance of control.

In an age of confusion and cynicism, such psychic resources can prove valuable. Ronald Reagan's speech following the Challenger crash is one example of the value of the shamanistic role. FDR's reassurances during the Depression provide another valuable model. This role can be powerful—but it is also open to abuse.

> **RARELY DO 'LEADERS' TRULY LEAD. USUALLY THEY FOLLOW, ARE COMPELLED TO GIVE THE PEOPLE WHAT THEY WANT AND DEMAND.**

An age of cynicism also opens the door for political outsiders to emerge as viable candidates for leadership. Just as the Depression spawned the emergence of some quirky and/or extremist power seekers and gave them some bit of credibility, so too do the events of the past forty years give credibility to candidates who, in less trying times, would not be taken very seriously. In the aftermath of Vietnam, the previously discredited Richard Nixon is reborn. In the wake of Watergate, outsider Jimmy Carter captures the presidency; after the imperiled presidencies of Ford and Carter, outsider Ronald Reagan becomes president. And in more recent years, H. Ross Perot, another quirky political outsider, becomes a viable presidential candidate, capturing 19 percent of the vote in 1992. Our willingness to let outsiders become officeholders, while it does have a certain appeal, is also prone to danger as semi-amateurs (Carter, Reagan) end up becoming president, uninformed of the ways of Washington and therefore perhaps more mistake-prone.

An age of cynicism also opens up the possibility of a search for heroic leadership in its best and worst sense. While it is more common in a cynical age to tear down leaders (much of the intrusive Starr investigation into President Clinton's sex life falls into this category), there is also the possibility of blind hero worship and of succumbing to a "true-believer" complex.

With such danger signs looming ahead, can we empower leaders to serve the larger public interest? Or must we succumb to this cynical age?

What is the foundation on which to build leadership in a cynical age? The steps are vexing: rebuild trust, educate the people, appeal to our better angels, build hope, and honor public service

What insights can we gain about the presidency from this examination of leadership in an age of cynicism? First, it reinforces the view that leadership (presidential and otherwise) is almost wholly contextual. Therefore, second, to be effective, leaders must bring a wide array of skills and styles to the task of governing, so as to (third) style-flex—adjust the leadership style to the demands of the situation. Fourth, the bully pulpit and symbolic roles of a president are essential components of leadership. Fifth, while leaders inherit a set of conditions, those conditions are not immutable; leaders can—to a degree—change the content.

This research reinforces several themes often discussed in the literature on political leadership. First, it supports the view that there is not one leadership style for all seasons. Second, leadership is largely contextual or situational, and the effective leader is adept at matching his/her leadership style to the demands/needs of the time/situation. Third, well-rounded leaders must have the capacity to "style-flex" and not be rigidly married to any single style of leadership. Fourth, because conditions change (often rapidly), electing a leader because he fits one need does not mean that the leader has the capacity to shift styles when conditions change. Fifth, while often neglected, leaders can fulfill (in part) the moral/spiritual needs of a community as national shaman. And finally, this research shows that leaders can matter.

In a cynical age, it may seem politically dangerous to venture into these forbidden areas, speak truth to power, challenge and prod, and ask for sacrifices. Do we serve others or merely ourselves?

Listen to the voice of the poet Bob Dylan:

> *Come senators, congressmen*
> *Please heed the call*
> *Don't stand in the doorway*
> *Don't block up the hall*
> *For he that gets hurt*
> *Will be he who has stalled*
> *There's a battle outside*
> *And it is ragin'.*
> *It'll soon shake your windows*
> *And rattle your walls*
> *For the times they are a-changin'.'*

MICHAEL A. GENOVESE holds the Loyola Chair of Leadership Studies and is a professor of political science at Loyola Marymount University in Los Angeles, California. He has published eleven books, most recently, *The Power of the American Presidency, 1789-2000,* Oxford University Press, 2001. He is currently editing *The Encyclopedia of the American Presidency* for Facts On File.

[1] Kryzanek, Michael. (1999). *Angry, Bored, Confused: A Citizen Handbook of American Politics.* Boulder, CO: Westview; Euchner, Charles C. (1996). *Extraordinary Politics: How Protest and Dissent are Changing American Democracy.* Boulder, CO: Westview.

[2] Wills, Gary. (1999). *A Necessary Evil: A History of Distrust of Government.* New York: Simon & Schuster.

[3] Dionne, E. J. (1991). *Why Americans Hate Politics.* New York: Simon & Schuster.

[4] Esler, Gavin. (1997). *The United States of Anger.* New York: Penguin.

[5] Nelson, Michael. (1995). *Why Americans Hate Politics and Politicians.* PS: Political Science & Politics, Mar.

[6] Esler, Gavin. (1997). *The United States of Anger.* New York: Penguin.

[7] Tolchin, Susan J. (1988). *The Angry American: How Voter Rage is Changing the Nation.* Boulder, CO: Westview.

[8] Genovese, Michael A. (1999). *The Watergate Crisis.* Westport, CT: Greenwood.

[9] Ginsberg, Benjamin and Shafter, Martin. (1996). *Politics by Other Means.* New York: Basic Books.

[10] Bennett, W. Lance. (1998). *The Uncivic Culture: Community, Identity, and the Rise of Lifestyle Politics.* PS: Political Science and Politics, Dec.

[11] Putnam, Robert D. (1995). *Tuning in, Tuning Out: The Strange Disappearance of Social Capital in America.* PS: Political Science and Politics, Dec.

[12] Bennett, W. Lance. (1998). *The Uncivic Culture: Community, Identity, and the Rise of Lifestyle Politics.* PS: Political Science and Politics, Dec.

[13] Kutler, Stanley. (1990). *The Wars of Watergate.* New York: Knopf; Emery, Fred. (1994). *Watergate.* New York: Touchstone.

[14] Genovese, Michael A. (1990). *The Nixon Presidency: Power and Politics in Turbulent Times.* Westport, CT: Greenwood.

[15] Marty, Martin E. (1998). *The Hateful Season.* The Los Angeles Times, Dec. 27.

[16] Ibid., Marty.

[17] Ibid., Marty.

[18] Craig, Stephen C., ed. (1995). *Broken Contract? Changing Relationships Between Americans and their Government.* Boulder, CO: Westview.

[19] Barry Glassner. (1999). *The Culture of Fear: The Assault on Optimism in America.* New York: Basic Books.

[20] Lerner, Michael. (1996). *The Politics of Meaning: Restoring Hope and Possibility in an Age of Cynicism.* Boulder, CO: Perseus.

[21] Cronin, Thomas E. and Genovese, Michael A. (1998). *The Paradox of the American Presidency.* New York: Oxford University Press.

Cashing in on Machiavelli

By Michael Jackson

"Alas, we who wished to lay the foundations of kindness could not ourselves be kind."
— Bertold Brecht, "To Posterity"

LIKE A RESTLESS SPIRIT FROM THE ABYSS, NICCOLÒ MACHIAVELLI rises from the deep at the beck of authors, editors and publishers. A few titles make the point: *The Greening of Machiavelli: the Evolution of International Environmental Politics* (1994), *Dear Prince, the unexpurgated counsels of N. Machiavelli to Richard Milhouse Nixon* (1969), *Tennis by Machiavelli* (1985), and *A Child's Machiavelli: A Primer on Power* (1998). There are also CD-ROM games entitled *Machiavelli*. There is nothing new in this invocation; H. G. Wells did it in *The New Machiavelli* (1911). In addition, there are all those books on management and leadership with Machiavelli's name in the title or subtitle, like *The Boss: Machiavelli on Managerial Leadership* (2000), *The Mafia Manager: A Guide to the Corporate Machiavelli* (1997), and *Machiavelli: Renaissance Real Politik for Modern Managers* (1997). Why is the soul of this minor functionary and amateur writer denied eternal rest?

The profusion of titles supports the conclusion that authors, editors and publishers suppose that book buyers and readers know something of Machiavelli. Only on that assumption would they take his name. More thought is likely given to the title of a mass-market book than to anything else, apart from the cover. While many other spirits are called to lend authority to books on leadership, few are called as often as Machiavelli. It would seem that many intelligent people who know a lot about book publishing and selling have decided that the name Machiavelli has market recognition.

In the pages that follow, this paper will:

(1) set forth in part the vulgar interpretation of Machiavelli that dominates the leadership titles in which his name appears,

(2) place that interpretation in the context of Machiavelli's reputation for evil,

(3) compare that reputation with the arguments found in Machiavelli's texts,

(4) offer a more subtle interpretation of Machiavelli's political theory of leadership, and

(5) draw some conclusions.

Vulgar Machiavellianism

The themes in the trade and mass-market books taking Machiavelli's name are clear and simple. It is a simplicity and a clarity that has become a stereotype.

They include realism—see the world as it is, immorality. Others are unscrupulous so act first, instrumentalism—ends justify means, and manipulation —use any means to influence others. That rehearsal suffices for a moment.

Before proceeding to details, let us pause to consider a parallel between what was once called Vulgar Marxism and Vulgar Machiavellianism. Vulgar Marxism simplified the many and complex arguments of Karl Marx into a few iron laws of historical determinism, focusing on the consequences Marx foretold rather than the dynamic, and contradictory process of history that unfolds those consequences. To illustrate, in the Vulgate, Marx predicted the revolution of workers. Workers did not revolt. Therefore, Marx erred. So it was that critics would focus on a few pages in the polemic of *The Communist Manifesto* to debunk a complex, detailed, empirical argument spread over hundreds of pages in *Das Capital* and the *Grundrisse* and the many other works. "Vulgar" does not mean rude, impolite, or uneducated. Many intellectuals of renown have settled for a vulgar interpretation of Karl Marx, witness Karl Popper's *The Open Society and Its Enemies* (1946). In Machiavelli's case, allies, not enemies, are the Vulgarians.

The comparison to Vulgar Marxism recommends itself for a second, more superficial reason. Machiavelli chose to write *The Prince* in Italian rather than in learned Latin, which was the common choice of intellectuals in his day, because it was the universal language of learning. For example, his contemporary Thomas More wrote *Utopia* in Latin rather than in the Vulgar English. In this usage 'vulgar' means the language spoken by common people who are not educated.

What is Vulgar Machiavellianism? It has three main elements. First and most generally, it reduces the subtlety and complexity of Machiavelli's arguments and applies them to contexts other than those he had in mind. Machiavelli studied, worked in, wrote about and was obsessed by politics. He did not have in mind business, tennis, environment, management or anything else. Machiavelli devoted himself to politics because it is the fundament of society. Aristotle defined the polity as the community of communities, the community that included all other human associations. Machiavelli went beyond that analytic claim to argue that the polity is necessary for all other forms of human association possible. It enables all other forms of civil association by providing external security and internal good order. To create these conditions for all other social life, politics is unique. It cannot be bound by or understood by the norms of the civil life it makes possible.

The first and most general vulgarization of Machiavelli paints his insights, epigrams, arguments and conclusions about politics onto other domains from sports to business. Writers exaggerate sports and business into life-and-death struggles and use these cartoons to justify brushing Machiavelli over the surface. Only those who have never been in combat would mistake corporate downsizing for a life-and-death struggle. It will be important later to note that Machiavelli treats war separately from politics. The rules of politics he distilled he did not apply directly to war, though some Vulgarians do. The approach described in this paragraph can be found in *Machiavelli on Modern Leadership* (1999), *Machiavelli on Management* (1991), and *The New Machiavelli: Renaissance Real Politick* (1997), among others.

The second vulgarization is to distort his teaching into the justification of means by ends. It follows from the preceding paragraph that for Machiavelli only one end justified immoral ends, and that is the foundation and perpetuation of a stable polity. Ends do not justify other means, nor do other ends justify immoral means. Put differently, Machiavelli did argue that the foundation of polity justified immoral means. That acknowledgement won for him the reputation of evil in the 16th century, a reputation that is traded on today. There is no general license for evil in Machiavelli. As will emerge below, he argues that evil is necessary but it remains evil. I shall also suggest that Machiavelli may flatter princes in order to deceive them, and that may deceive readers looking for the most superficial meaning of *The Prince*. Examples of books that generalize Machiavelli's political teaching include *The Mafia Manager* (1991), *The Boss: Machiavelli on Managerial Leadership* (2000), and *The Boss: A Contemporary Rendering of the Prince* (1986).

The third vulgarization of Machiavelli reduces his theory to quotations and uses them as decoration. That these quotations might together form a context that endows each with a meaning is neglected in this Bartlett's approach. Sometimes Machiavelli's chapter titles are used; other times quotations are sprinkled through an otherwise conventional management text. In some cases Machiavelli's name appears on the title page and then disappears from the text. See *The New Prince* (1999), *The Princessa: Machiavelli for Women* (1997), and *Management and Machiavelli* (1974).

Machiavelli's Reputation for Evil

Within a generation of the publication of *The Prince*, Machiavelli had the posthumous reputation for evil. While Thomas More in *Utopia* recommended assassination, mercenaries, slavery, and deceit, he went on to become a saint. How and why Machiavelli was reduced to the devil's cipher is the text for another time and place. For the purposes at hand, what is relevant is that he courted this reputation by the direct manner in which he discussed deceit, violence and ambition. Previous writers had discussed these topics but always with a screen of moral judgment. Thomas More put his recommendations in the mouths of others and, in the last line of the book, ambiguously distanced himself from its content. Moreover, many in politics had long practiced what Machiavelli preached. What set Machiavelli apart was less the content than the clinical manner of analysis.

By 1599 Machiavelli was called the preacher of evil, and his book was proscribed on the Catholic Church's Index. By 1595 readers understood that "Machiavelli" was a synonym for evil in English.[1] Little changes. In 1995 *Machiavelli for Beginners* portrays the Florentine with the horns of a devil.[2] In five hundred years *The Prince* had traveled from blasphemy to cliché.

The Prince is a slim volume of little more than one hundred pages.[3] It is presented as advice to a prince, which was a well-established *genre* of the day.

> Machiavelli says his purpose and method in express words. Many have imagined republics and principalities which have never in truth been known to exist; the gulf between how one should live and how one does live is so wide that a man who neglects what is done learns the way to self destruction.[4]

Note that Machiavelli does not disparage normative thinking, thinking about "how one should live." Nor does he imply that there is an unbridgeable gulf between how one should live and how one does live. He predicts danger if one concentrates solely on how one should live.

Elsewhere he said: *"I believe that the true way of understanding the road to Paradise is to know that of hell in order to avoid the latter."*[5] Again he is precise. He makes a personal commitment to find "the road to Paradise" by carefully avoiding the road to hell. He does not say that avoiding the road to hell is Paradise. Knowing the road to hell, we may better pursue that to Paradise. The geography of the two roads is complementary, not mutually exclusive.

Together these two passages are the basis for his reputation as a realist. Life contains a road to hell and it has to be examined, the better to avoid it. If this is what "realism" means, then call Machiavelli a realist. Francis Bacon then was right in 1605 to say that, "We are beholden to Machiavelli and others who wrote of what men do and not what they ought to do."[6] However, "realism" is often given a more specific meaning, having to do with self-interest and the ruthless and relentless advancement of self-interest. That meaning goes well beyond the text we have of Machiavelli.

The *genre* of letters to Christian princes that *The Prince* parodies is full of fanciful recommendations, as if praying it is so would make it so.[7] Others had recognized the need to see the world as it is, but again Machiavelli is distinctive for being unapologetic about it in what is after all a book he did not publish. Had he surrounded the text of *The Prince* we have with the ritual apologies and excuses of other writers, he might well have both escaped his reputation and our notice.

Machiavelli, *The Prince* and a prince

The Prince circulated in manuscript within the year of its completion. It was published in 1532 after his death. Machiavelli only published one book in his lifetime, *The Art of War.*

Machiavelli wrote *The Prince* in exile outside Florence. He had served as third Chancellor in a republican government of the city. His service included foreign missions, which made him aware of Italy's low standing among the major powers of the day like France. When the de Medici family seized the government again, Machiavelli was dismissed, tortured and exiled. Not all servants of the republic survived, while others remained in office. Why Machiavelli escaped death but suffered torture may be fortune.[8]

Though many of the mediums who commune with Machiavelli's shade extol the acumen of his insights into how to manipulate others in *The Prince,* and buttress this conviction with reference to his own political career, inevitably exaggerated into something more important than it was, few acknowledge either:

(1) that he was a failure, neither gaining high office nor influencing events, and

(2) he could not persuade the one man he is routinely supposed to have tried to persuade to rehabilitate him, namely the dedicatee of *The Prince,* Lorzeno de Medici. The cunning fallen angel of Vulgar Machiavellianism would surely have taken his own advice and succeeded.

Machiavelli affixed to *The Prince* a dedication to the new Medici prince of Florence.[9] In this dedication Machiavelli says that the short book following contains all he knows about politics. Many conclude from that dedication that Machiavelli wrote the book to win the favor of Prince Medici. That conclusion attains strength when we note that Machiavelli said as much in letters. Yet the truth may be more variegated, for he made little effort in the remaining twelve years of his life to submit the book to Prince Medici. Moreover, while he wrote *The Prince,* he also wrote another, larger book called *The Discourses on the First Ten Books of Titus Livius's History of Rome,* known as *The Discourses.* This book is of a different order, and when it is taken into account a more whole Machiavelli emerges, and the context in which we may best understand *The Prince* enlarges. According to his correspondence he broke off writing *The Discourses* to compose *The Prince,* as though this shorter book was relief from the historical commentary of *The Discourses.*[10] That circumstantial evidence alone braids together *The Prince* and *The Discourses* as vine to fence.

Since Jean-Jacques Rousseau in the 18th century, at least, theorists have seen the republican stripes on Machiavelli's shoulders, even if authors, editors and publishers of mass market books have not, and theorists have reconciled *The Prince* with that insignia.[11] Rousseau's conclusion is that Machiavelli taught that we are free politically to make our own fate and that is the single overriding and radical message of *The Prince.*[12] Contemporary scholars offer more complicated interpretations of contextual evidence to arrive at the same conclusion.[13] While some hammer Machiavelli into clichés, scholars conserve a many-sided Machiavelli.

In these pages two other of Machiavelli's works appear. *The Art of War,* the book he published in 1521, is one. The other is a play he wrote for private amusement, *The Mandrake.* He wrote poems and plays as well as essays. *The Mandrake* illustrates the political theory contained in *The Prince* and *The Discourses.*

The unity of *The Prince* and *The Discourses* deepens with an obvious parallel. Both books start with a letter of dedication. That of *The Discourses* also says it contains all Machiavelli knows.[14] It is dedicated to two republican leaders of Florence. *The Discourses* appeared posthumously, too, in 1531.

The two books were written at the same time over a two-year period. Both have dedications declaring that each book spans Machiavelli's knowledge of politics. The books are, respectively, dedicated to a prince and to republicans. Is one declaration true and the other false? Is one dedication literal and the other a jest? Or are both dedications true, and do the dedications offer a clue as to how to merge *The Prince* and *The Discourses?* It is the latter question that informs these pages, an interpretation confirmed by reference to *The Art of War* and *The Mandrake.*

In *The Prince,* the high politics of foundation and perpetuation of a community rests on savage and violent acts. Romulus killed his brother Remus to found Rome. That is an act of foundation. These acts are beyond the pale of morality, as Machiavelli recognizes. At the same time, *The Discourses* emphasizes the importance of morality in private life within a secure polity. The high politics of foundation and perpetuation goes beyond conventional morality in order to make conventional morality possible. This theme will be expanded upon below.

Politics has a logic of its own, according to Machiavelli. This point cannot be overemphasized. It alone forecloses nearly all of Vulgar Machiavellianism on leadership. His subject is the politics of survival in a world without order. His subject is not football, tennis, commercial success, office holding or gaining, or anything else. As decisive and glorious as Al "Chainsaw" Dunlop's business career was, it had nothing to do with the foundation and perpetuation of a secure civil society in which ordinary persons might live and work. Such a comparison misses the point of *The Prince*. Still less is his subject this or that policy or program.

In Chapter 15 of *The Prince,* where the first reference to "imagined republics" occurs, Machiavelli says that "a man who wants to act virtuously in every way necessarily comes to grief among so *many* who are not virtuous."[15] It is a passage repeatedly quoted in the Vulgar Machiavellian literature, often to attribute some general view of human nature to Machiavelli. It is then a passage that repays examination.

> **" MACHIAVELLI SAYS THAT BECAUSE OF THE FICKLENESS OF SUBJECTS A PRINCE CAN BE HATED FOR DOING GOOD AS READILY AS FOR DOING EVIL. EXPERIENCED POLITICIANS WILL NOD SADLY AT THE TRUTH OF THIS OBSERVATION. "**

Note that it refers to "a man," but it occurs in a chapter on "How a prince should govern." It would seem this is not just any "man" but a prince. If a prince wants to act virtuously in every way the prince will necessarily come to grief among so many who are not virtuous. This passage supports the conclusion that a prince may act virtuously very often, but not in every way.

Nor does Machiavelli say in this passage that all (men and women) are vicious rather than virtuous. He says that a prince acts amongst "so *many* who are not virtuous" inside the fatal circle of life. Even that may exceed the needs of the argument. Machiavelli need only argue that the prince moves in circles where there may be vicious individuals and that it is not possible to ascertain with confidence who is vicious and who is virtuous. To survive in that world, the prince is advised to act prudently on the assumption that others are vicious.

There is more. Acting on the assumption that others are vicious does not come easily. Machiavelli counsels that a prince must "*learn* how not to be virtuous."[16] This passage underscores Machiavelli's commitment to conventional morality.

Still more can be added to the picture. In Chapter 19, on the need for the prince to avoid incurring the hatred of subjects, Machiavelli says that because of the fickleness of subjects a prince can be hated for doing good as readily as for doing evil. Experienced politicians will nod sadly at the truth of this observation. In politics "a prince is … often forced not to be good."[17] Forced.

The evil attributed to Machiavelli is unnatural, according to Machiavelli. It must be learned, and sometimes it is forced on a prince. Scarcely Satan's consul?

Earlier in *The Prince*, Machiavelli recounts the story of Agathocles of Syracuse, a contemporary of Hannibal. Agathocles was a decisive man of action who did not hesitate to use violence. Machiavelli praises Agathocles for his decisiveness for a page, and then he adds: "Yet it cannot be called prowess to kill fellow citizens, to betray friends, to be treacherous, pitiless, irreligious."[18] Why ever not? Is this not exactly what the devil would commend? More important, why does it matter if only ends count? Machiavelli's answer is that, "These ways can win power but not glory." He goes on to condemn Agathocles for his "brutal cruelty, in humanity, his countless crimes, which altogether forbid his being honored among eminent men." In this passage, Machiavelli trades his white clinical lab coat for a judge's black robes to pass a verdict. Is this the devil's work?

Machiavelli's criticism of Agathocles shows the levels of his judgment. On the one hand, Agathocles was courageous and decisive, and those are necessary qualities. On the other hand, Agathocles went beyond what was necessary for the security of the regime. Necessity marks the extent of a prince's writ. Not everything is permitted by *raison d'état*, which is why it is called *raison d'état*. Necessity can be judged by *raison,* and the limit is the needs of *l'état.*

Machiavelli distils his political theory in a passage that follows when he says violence may be used well where it is used once and for all. He repeats this point in the next paragraph for emphasis: "violence should be inflicted once and for all."[19] Later commentaries have called this the economy of violence.[20] Violence is used to end conflicts, not to settle scores or for mere sport.

Machiavelli's Political Theory

Reading *The Prince* and *The Discourses* together reveals the whole of Machiavelli's political theory. A prince founds and secures a polis. That requires rising above conventional morality. Once the polity is secure, citizens will depose the prince and install a republican government of equals.

As the supreme political actor engaged in the highest political act of creating a stable regime, the prince may exceed conventional morality. The prince is a means to an end. In this sense he is a transitional figure and a transactional leader. He offers to supporters the achievement of specified conditions. Once those conditions have been achieved, followers no longer need the prince. This latter point is however discreetly omitted from *The Prince*. If *The Prince* is a book about deception, it is also a book that might deceive a princely reader.

The Prince has deceived many readers. Coming to it with prejudices derived from Machiavelli's reputation for evil, they note only the crudest arguments. *(Here speaks a teacher frustrated with these prejudices in undergraduates.)* They read the book quickly and superficially, much as a prince might do, a man of action with no time for the split hairs of academia.

> **THOSE WHO HAVE LEARNED TO USE DIRTY HANDS WHEN IT IS NECESSARY MAY KEEP USING THEM WHEN IT IS NOT. THE BLOOD MAY BLIND THEM TO THE LIMIT OF NECESSITY.**

Machiavelli's argument is heavily qualified. It would be better if a sensible and sane person, not Agathocles, took on the task of princely foundation. Hence, the discussion of *learning* how not to be good, and being *forced* to use violence.

It is unlikely that a sane and sensible person will accept the responsibility of princely foundation. Rarely is a morally good person willing to do what a prince may have to do — to live in an uncertain world, surrounded by the ambitious. Machiavelli's prince is like the Communist leader Hoerderer in Jean-Paul Sartre's play *Dirty Hands*. "I have dirty hands right up to the elbow. I've plunged them in filth and blood. Do you think I can govern innocently?"[21] Machiavelli would not think such a man could govern innocently, and that might be a reason why such a man should not govern in peaceful times.

Those who have learned to use dirty hands when it is necessary may keep using them when it is not. The blood may blind them to the limit of necessity. Successful revolutionaries may find it difficult to solve problems with pens after years of solving them with guns. Aware of this, some revolutionary movements distinguish the military and political side of the movement, e.g., ETA, IRA, and the Mau Mau. The partition confines dirty hands and the immorality that goes with them to a few. Overall, Machiavelli points to a distinct set of political methods and strategies which good men must study, not only because their use does not come naturally, but also because they are explicitly condemned by the moral teachings good men accept, concludes Michael Walzer.[22] As Hannah Arendt put it, politics has one morality and life another.[23] The former makes the latter possible.

The good person who aims to found or reform a republic must do terrible things. Rarely will a good person be willing to use these methods.[24]

Walzer contrasts Machiavelli's prince with Max Weber's politician and Albert Camus's revolutionaries.[25] These two leaders are endowed with more psychological depth than Machiavelli imparts to the prince. Whereas the only moral limit on the prince is necessity, Weber's politician is limited by the personal capacity to bear guilt. No doubt most good people would feel so much guilt they would not be able to meet Machiavelli's criterion of necessity. Though some might be able to meet and even surpass it.

The revolutionaries that Camus imagines in "The Just Assassins" respect necessity and feel guilt, but they also limit their actions by the capacity of followers to understand and endure the pain of violence. This constraint is recognized in the willingness of the revolutionaries to accept punishment for their crimes. Crimes? Killing innocent people is a crime even if it is necessary. This is Camus's argument, and it is one with which Machiavelli would agree.

The kind of end-means analysis implicit in Machiavelli is sometimes taken for utilitarianism. Among all the varieties of utilitarianism there is agreement on one point. Jeremy Bentham, John Stuart Mill, Henry Sidgwick, Richard Hare, Jack Smart, all place life outside the utilitarian calculus. Necessity is beyond the comfort of a utilitarian calculus.[26]

In a seminar room, intellectuals may debate the definition of "necessity" but in Machiavelli's Italy this luxury was irrelevant. Necessity included an end to foreign invasions, safety of limb and life, security of property, personal safety in one's home and on the street.

If Machiavelli's purpose is to advocate that the ends justify the means in politics, there would be no need for him to argue that a prince must *learn* how not to be good, and may be *forced* to be bad. If the ends justify the means, there is nothing left to justify morally. If instrumental success is the only criterion and if the means achieve the end, then there is nothing immoral about it. That Machiavelli describes high politics as *learning* how not to be good, being *forced* to be bad reveals his own belief that the violence of high politics is immoral yet it must be done.

"The act accuses, the result excuses" is a passage from *The Discourses* often cited. Once again the full text makes clear that Machiavelli is making a very limited point:

[A] wise man will never criticize someone for an extralegal action under-taken to organize a kingdom or to establish a republic. He will agree if the act accuses, the results excuse … for it is those who are violent to destroy who should be found guilty, not those who are violent in order to build anew.[27]

The only end that justifies violent means is that which organizes a kingdom or estab-lishes a republic. Both of these are high standards. Of course, Machiavelli may be mistaken in supposing that violence can stop further violence, but the point remains that he offers no license to murder and mayhem. Something of Machiavelli's attitude toward political violence can be seen in his estimate of mercenaries.

> **THAT MACHIAVELLI DESCRIBES HIGH POLITICS AS *LEARNING* HOW NOT TO BE GOOD, BEING *FORCED* TO BE BAD REVEALS HIS OWN BELIEF THAT THE VIOLENCE OF HIGH POLITICS IS IMMORAL YET IT MUST BE DONE.**

Mercenaries were common in the 16th century.[28] They were the profession-al soldiers in an age without professional armies. Machiavelli's attitude toward mer-cenaries belies some of the incantations of Vulgar Machiavellianism. His contem-porary, Thomas More, enthusiastically recommends the use of mercenaries in *Utopia*—they come cheap; better that they suffer and die than Utopians.[29] Now that is a hardheaded, hard-hearted, calculating, and ruthless prescription—exactly what Machiavelli should commend in Vulgar Machiavellianism, but he does not. Instead he says mercenaries "are useless and dangerous."[30]

In *The Art of War,* Machiavelli's critique of mercenaries has two sides.[31] Machiavelli contends that mercenaries are unreliable, incompetent, untrustworthy, and expensive. This is the criticism of practicality. It is a critique based on the close observation of mercenaries in Italy in his time.

He says profit and glory animate mercenaries, things that they can only enjoy if they live to tell the tale. These incentives reduce their ardor for the bloody work of war. They accept public contracts to defend or attack, make a great show of noise, color, smoke, and dust while agreeing among themselves who is to win on the day and how to share the money. It is all rather like those gladiatorial contests broadcast on television these days: entertainment with war paint, sub-verbal grunts, bulging muscles, and choreographed fisticuffs and pratfalls. Machiavelli concluded that mercenaries could not be trusted to guard the liberty of a city. They would not die gloriously in battle for the patrimony.

The second side of his critique is that the use of mercenaries meant citizens were unwilling to defend the polity themselves. That unwillingness is a sure sign of corruption for Machiavelli.

Citizens of a healthy polity possessed of civic virtue are willing and able to defend it. It is another of Machiavelli's insights that peace and war form a continuum. Whereas later theorists like Thomas Hobbes and John Locke juxtapose peace and war as alternatives, Machiavelli reflects one in the other. *The Art of War* is a detailed program for raising, equipping and training a citizen militia.

Machiavelli longs for heroic citizens of Roman mythology who would gladly die for the hilltop of their birth. Here is Machiavelli the romantic. His images are ancient Romans of myth. Pericles's funeral oration captures the meaning Machiavelli had in mind, the noble death in battle, the classical monuments to educate successors on their duties, the dignified survivors, and the fitting words of a statesman.[32] Roman history does tell of heroes but it also tells of many scoundrels, and Machiavelli neglects most of the latter.

Machiavelli's greatest romantic wish was for a united and stable Italy, an unrealistic ambition in his day, and one realized only three hundred years later. Hardly the cold-eyed realist. In the last chapter of *The Prince,* he invokes the image of an Italia rampant to deliver Italians from invaders.[33] An image of *Italia* adorned the walls of his office in the chancellery and is still to be seen. The road to Paradise leads to *Italia.*

The final piece of the puzzle of Machiavelli's political theory is the vantage point afforded by his comic play *The Mandrake.*[34] In this play, a wily schemer arranges a marriage that secures a fortune, bringing stability to the community. The only two characters in the play who understand the larger picture of stability are the schemer and the woman who accepts the subterfuge for her own purposes. Libido, avarice, and vanity blind the two men in her life.

Those eager to extend Machiavelli's teaching beyond politics may cite this play to contend that Machiavelli did so himself.[35] Yet in the play the focus is on the stability of community, not on desires of any of the characters. In addition, there is no violence in the play. It was the fashion in the 1970s to say that the personal was the political. At the time, that assertion opened the way for analysis and argument of important matters. Some take that assertion as a permit to render Machiavelli's teaching general. That would be an anachronistic reading of Machiavelli, reading the concerns of today back into these books. The personal may be the political for us, but it was not for Machiavelli.

The Mandrake shows Machiavelli's recognition that the good of the whole is possible. It has to be created, not assumed. To create it takes deceit, bribes, and the like; these immoralities are justified so long as they are in proportion to the end achieved in politics. Machiavelli's concentration on the high politics of foundation and perpetuation distinguish him from many political theorists like Thomas More who assume foundation but do not consider how it is achieved.

Conclusion

The prince is a transactional leader, offering to overcome personal inhibitions to do what is necessary to create a polity. Because it is unlikely that a scrupulous person will be able and willing to overcome all inhibitions, the prince is more likely Richard III than Prince Hal, more likely someone already unscrupulous rather than one to be reborn in office. Though it would be anachronistic to call it a contract, the analogy of an implicit bargain makes the point. The people endure the prince for the foundation of order. They can understand the need for a prince by reading *The Prince,* and they can learn when a prince is no longer needed by reading *The Discourses.* Once order is achieved, subjects must transform themselves into citizens —particularly by willing the perpetuation of their society in its military defense. In time they will supplant the prince and make a republic.

There is another reason why Machiavelli's *The Prince* remains an attractive book, especially to those thinking about leadership. Machiavelli's conceit is that the person matters. Though social science surrendered the idea of the hero in history generations ago and embraced structure over agency as the level of explanation, the importance of the individual remains intuitively attractive, and Machiavelli acts as a lightning rod for that sentiment. The prince he imagines is an event-making person, not just an eventful person.[36] That is the sense in which Rousseau said Machiavelli is the teacher of freedom.

Many books of Vulgar Machiavellianism are well written, insightful and provocative on leadership and management. My objection is solely that Machiavelli sheds no light on anything but political leadership, and none of these books shares that exclusive focus. They merge sports, business, war and politics as though all are on the same plane. To Machiavelli, they are not one.

If clairvoyants did produce Machiavelli at a séance on a wet afternoon, there is no doubt that he would be very amused to find he is a figure of controversy these five hundred years later. What a joke! Which would amuse him more? The invocations of Vulgar Machiavellianism or my own pompous efforts to dignify him, no one knows. Machiavelli would laugh.

MICHAEL JACKSON, Ph.D., is a professor of government and international relations and associate dean of the Faculty of Economics and Business at the University of Sydney in Australia.

[1] We know a lot about Machiavelli's life. At the height of political office he would spend his evening in the company of Cicero, Seneca, Plato, and their kind, as he studied their books, he says in a letter. See Peter Bondanella and Mark Musa, *The Portable Machiavelli* (Harmondsworth: Penguin, 1979, p. 69). His books are peopled with noble Romans of the Republic. We have nearly everything he wrote. There are no missing works. He wrote in a clear and simple Italian, which was what first brought him to the attention of superiors in government service; there are no codes or gaps for scholars to interpret. In addition to the manuscripts he wrote, we have many letters that are consistent with the works. See Roberto Ridolfi, *The Life of Machiavelli* (London: Routledge & Kegan Paul, 1963) and James Atkinson and David Sices, *Machiavelli and His Friends: Their Personal Correspondence* (DeKalb: Northern Illinois University Press, 1996). Specifically on his reputation, see Felix Rabb, *The English Face of Machiavelli* (London: Routledge & Kegan Paul, 1964) and Friedrich Meinecke, *Machiavellianism* (London: Routledge & Kegan Paul, 1957 [1927]).

[2] Curry, Patrick and Zarate, Oscar. (1995). *Machiavelli for Beginners.* Cambridge: Icon.

[3] For the purposes at hand, the Penguin translation suffices. It is inexpensive and readily available editions like it that influence most readers.

[4] Machiavelli, Niccolo. (1961). *The Prince.* Harmondsworth: Penguin, p. 91. Machiavelli was partly reacting to the rediscovery of Plato in the Florence of his time. See also Brown, Alison. (1986). Platonism in Fifteenth Century Florence and Its Contribution to Early Modern Political Thought. *Journal of Modern History,* 58, 2, pp. 383-413.

[5] From a letter in Bondanella and Musa, *The Portable Machiavelli,* p. 74.

[6] Bacon, Francis, *The Advancement of Learning,* xxi, 9.

[7] Skinner, Quentin. *The Foundations of Modern Political Thought.* Cambridge: Cambridge University Press. p.177ff.

[8] In addition to Ridolfi, *The Life of Niccolò Machiavelli,* see also De Grazia, Sebastian. *Machiavelli in Hell.* London:Harvester.

[9] Machiavelli. *The Prince,* p. 29.

[10] Bondanella and Musa, *The Portable Machiavelli,* p. 69. *The Prince* itself contains an allusion to *The Discourses* on its opening page, p. 33.

[11] Hexter, Jack. (1964). The Loom on Language and the Fabric of Imperatives: The Case of *Il Principe* and *Utopia. American Historical Review,* p. 949.

[12] Rousseau, Jean-Jacques. (1978) *On the Social Contract.* Masters, Roger, ed. New York: St. Martins. Book III, chapter VI.

[13] Mattingly, Garrett. (1958). Machiavelli's Prince. *American Scholar,* 27:483; Wolin, Sheldon. (1960). *Politics and Vision.* Boston: Little Brown. p. 231; and Dietz, Mary. (1986). Trapping the Prince. *American Political Science Review,* 80, 3, pp. 777-799. See also Mansfield, Harvey, Jr. *Taming the Prince.* University of Chicago Press.

[14] Machiavelli. (1970). *The Discourses.* Harmondsworth: Penguin, p. 93.

[15] Machiavelli, *The Prince,* p. 91.

[16] *Ibid.*

[17] *Ibid.,* p. 108.

[18] *Ibid.,* p. 62.

[19] *Ibid.,* p. 66.

[20] Sheldon Wolin coined this phrase in *Politics and Vision,* p. 220.

[21] Sartre, Jean-Paul. Dirty Hands. *No Exit and Three Other Plays.(1956).* trans. Lionel Abel. New York: Vintage, p. 224.

[22] Walzer, Michael. (1972). Political Action: The Problem of Dirty Hands. *Philosophy & Public Affairs,* 2: 168.

[23] Arendt, Hannah. Truth and Politics. In *Between Past and Future (1954).* New York: Viking, p. 235.

[24] Machiavelli, *The Discourses,* Book I, Chapter XVIII, p. 171.

[25] Weber, Max. Politics as a Vocation. Gerth, Hans & Mills, C. W., eds. (1927) *From Max Weber.* New York; Camus,

Albert. The Just Assassins. *No Exit and Three Other Plays. (1956)* Abel, Lionel, trans. New York: Vintage.

[26] For another fictional example, see Fowles, John. (1966). *The Magus.* London: Cape.

[27] Machiavelli, *The Discourses,* Book I, chapter IX, p. 139.

[28] Mallett, Michael. (1974). *Mercenaries and their Masters: Warfare in Renaissance Italy.* London: Bodly Head.

[29] More, Thomas. *Utopia.* Harmondsworth: Penguin, p. 85.

[30] Machiavelli, *The Prince,* p. 77.

[31] Machiavelli, *The Art of War.* Indianapolis: Bobbs-Merrill. This 1965 edition has a 100 page introduction by Neal Wood.

[32] Thucydides, *History of the Peloponnesian War,* Book II.

[33] Machiavelli, *The Prince,* pp. 133-138.

[34] Hulling, Mark. (1978). Machiavelli's Mandragola. *Review of Politics, 40:32-57;* Lukes, Timothy. (1981). Play Therapy in Political Theory: Machiavelli's Mandragola. *Teaching Political Science.* Sept. 1, pp. 35-38.

[35] Beiner, Ronald. Missionaries and Mercenaries. in *Cruelty & Deception: The Controversy over Dirty Hands in Politics. (1999).* Shugarman, David & Rynard, Paul, eds. Peterborough, Ont.: Broadview Press, p. 47.

[36] Hook, Sidney. (1992 first published 1945). *The hero in history : a study in limitation and possibility.* New Brunswick, USA: Transaction Publishers. See also Bloomhardt, Paul. (1941). *The Great Man in History.* Columbus: Ohio University Press.

Backing the Right Horse

Transactional vs. Transformational Leadership Of State Transitions: A Research Prospectus

By Mark Clarence Walker

WHAT FORM DOES SUCCESSFUL REFORM POLITICAL LEADERSHIP take for a country in transition to democracy? Is a different kind of leadership required for a transition to a market economy? Leadership plays a crucial role, along with specific policies and programs, in guiding the reform efforts of states. Transformational leaders are good at providing a vision of what should come next and motivating their followers to complete their shared goals. Transactional leaders are good at providing goods and services in exchange for legitimacy from the people. This paper will explore the hypothesis that transactional leaders make better reform leaders because they are better suited to carry out economic reforms.

This paper discusses how the need for market reform may trump the need for political reform in today's global economy. Many elites work under the assumption that political liberalization will necessarily follow economic liberalization. This paper will also discuss whether a democratic or authoritarian leader is more effective, or desired, to lead state reforms. In addition, is charisma necessary to successful reform leadership?

This study will bridge the gap between Leadership Studies, area studies, and formal political science. Rigorous methodology applied to the new laboratory of the Post-Communist states of Europe and Asia will help to unite the discipline of political science with the field of Leadership Studies and the area studies subfields which focus on non-U.S. parts of the world. The study of political leadership and of the Soviet Union, Russia, and the Russian Empire are of irrefutable importance; however, their study has been distanced from the discipline of political science because the application of rigorous methods to these fields has been problematic in the past. My study will show that these problems can be resolved and these studies united.

Importance

Why Certain Leaders are Supported in Domestic and International Policy Arenas

The importance of understanding this distinction goes beyond the academic as it sheds light on which leaders the international community and domestic constituents around the world should support in states attempting difficult reforms. During the Cold War both the United States and the Soviet Union supported power holders in countries in order to count them towards their bloc irrespective of their democratic or authoritarian nature.[1] The politics of the Cold War dominated all concerns—even economic ones. Since the Cold War, there has been a shift among international organizations and actors to support power holders in countries that they have the greatest confidence in to lead market reforms. The policies of the World Bank and the International Monetary Fund in the early 1990s are the best example of this shift.

There have also been demands from international organizations and actors for political liberalization to accompany market reform primarily based on the assumption that market reforms require a certain degree of liberal politics. However, the main focus has always been on securing economic reform gains first in transitioning countries. The predominant theory in policy circles governing how countries develop argues that political liberalization must follow economic liberalization; therefore, market reforms can be emphasized first while allowing various state regimes to remain authoritarian or even Communist. The U.S. decision to grant permanent most-favored-nation (MFN) status to China is the most prominent case of the application of this policy. Most U.S. policy elites argued that trading with China now will create help to create a middle class in China, introduce liberal ideas of governing, and begin fundamental changes in the society that will all culminate in the people demanding, and receiving, political liberalization.

Thus policy elites and international organizations have supported on the whole those power wielders who show the greatest promise for effectively managing market reforms. What kinds of leaders have these interests supported? Have these leaders been effective in managing market reforms or political liberalization efforts? These are some of the very important policy questions this paper will attempt to address.

Concerns in the Scholarly Literature

Political science as a discipline has had an ambivalent relationship with the study of leaders. Everyone understands that leaders play a central role in the study of political processes, institutions, behavior, and systems, but no one knows for sure exactly what that role is. Moreover, leadership may be one of the hardest topics to quantify and study with rigorous methodology; creativity, spontaneity and charisma often highlight many of the best examples of leadership.

This study, therefore, will contribute to the discipline of political science by clarifying the role leaders play in political processes and institutions by studying leadership with formal and quantitative methods. In particular this paper will focus on the role of leaders and leadership in transitioning states and societies and provide a template for *successful reform leadership*. This study will not ignore, however, the distinctive contribution of specific cases and will eventually include case studies that will provide texture to the theoretical nature of this study.

The study of leadership has gone through three distinct phases in the twentieth century. The first phase, which can be described as the Trait Period, lasted from 1910 until World War II. In this period scholars focused on characteristics they believed differentiated leaders from followers and thus gave leaders their abil-

> **" LEADERSHIP MAY BE ONE OF THE HARDEST TOPICS "
> TO QUANTIFY AND STUDY WITH RIGOROUS
> METHODOLOGY; CREATIVITY, SPONTANEITY AND
> CHARISMA OFTEN HIGHLIGHT MANY OF THE BEST
> EXAMPLES OF LEADERSHIP.**

ity to influence followers. The Behavior Period, coinciding with the general behavioralist movement in political science, lasted from World War II through at least the late 1960s. For Leadership Studies this meant that the study of different leadership styles became dominant. The most significant finding from this period was the distinction made between task-, or goal-, oriented leadership and people-oriented leadership ("people-persons"). The Contingency Period, which has lasted from the late 1960s until present day, has emphasized that leadership style alone is not important and that situational parameters matter.

An important area of Leadership Studies focuses on transactional or exchange theories of leadership. This literature highlights the considerable impact of the relationship between leaders and followers, and how followers legitimate leadership actions. Not only has this area been important for trying to understand how crimes against humanity are accomplished, for example by Hitler and the German people in the Holocaust, but this area has also simply put an emphasis on maybe the most important part of this process—the relationship between leaders and followers.

The major theoretical issues in the field of Leadership Studies coincide with the intellectual separation of the study of leaders from the broader study of politics within the discipline of political science. The study of leaders and followers must be reintegrated with the rest of political science in both the theoretical and disciplinary sense. The key to accomplishing this task is to study leadership with the methodological tools of political science—game theory, statistics, and rigorous conceptualization.

The intellectual separation I write of can be easily seen between the *area studies* subfields and the discipline of political science. The study of Soviet and Russian politics, for example, has often focused on the study of their leaders since World War II. While the discipline of political science was moving towards greater quantification, the study of various parts of the world outside of the United States consciously remained less *scientific.*

Today, however, *area studies* and Post-Communist Europe and Asia in particular present themselves as excellent laboratories for the study of political phenomena, especially leadership. The fall of Communism in Eurasia has presented several challenges from economic development to democratization in this region; however, the issue of effective governance of reform policies plays a central role in all of these challenges. My study therefore will help answer questions regarding what the best kind of leadership is to address effectively these challenges. In doing so, this study will necessarily be adding to the literatures on transition to democracy, Post-Soviet and East European studies, Leadership Studies, and comparative politics in general.

Research Methods

This study will use a comprehensive research design that includes formal theory, statistical analysis, data sets and case studies.[2] This study will include a set of formal models that describe the relationship between leaders and followers. Based on the idea that there are different types of authority and leaders, one set of models will describe the relationship between transformational leaders and their followers while another set will describe the relationship between transactional leaders and their followers. At best these models will help me to generate testable hypotheses. At worst these models will help me better to conceptualize the problem: for example, I must provide working definitions of *successful reform* and *successful reform leadership.* After generating several hypotheses, I will then test these propositions against my data. If I have a significant number of cases I will utilize some simple statistical methods in their analysis.

This study plans to organize the data into a large-N set of cases. These cases will be drawn from *all* of the countries experiencing state transition from Communism in Europe and Asia, including China and Vietnam. Therefore this study will necessarily be *comparative* in nature and will include cases of state transition *from authoritarian rule* and not just *to democracy* per se. Several in-depth case studies will be made on those cases that are either examples of different kinds of state transitions or simply illustrative of my hypotheses. My data will be expressed by statistics and by using a detailed description to get the stories of various leaders and transitions right. I expect the actual data *creation* and accumulation to be a significant part of my research task.

I will be conducting my research over a three-year period. I plan on dedicating the summer of 2000 and academic year 2000-2001 to research and writing on this project; most of my time, however, will be spent doing research. This research will be conducted using primary source material such as newspapers and archival documents. Interviews of important actors will also be sought but they will not be a primary focus of this project. Most of my time will be spent *getting the story right* for all of my cases and producing a large-N data set that summarizes various leaderships.

What Type of Leader Is Most Effective at the Reform of States?
Reform is Harder Than Revolution

In the last few decades, states in transition have usually chosen reform over revolution. Even states that have experienced nominal revolutions have also experienced periods in which they have needed to reform their institutions and society.[3] If any insights can be made about successful reform leadership, their significance would be assured given the importance of reform in today's world and the avoidance of the negative side effects that revolutions can spawn. What revolutions do best is destroy that which came before; they are not known for the institutions they build. In order for transitions from one system to another to be relatively smooth, irreversible, and lacking in extreme amounts of violence, leaders substitute new or reformed institutions, processes, ideas and actors for the old. Thus reform, and, consequently, reform leadership is particularly hard to do well (Burns, p. 169).

There are many reform leaders who have attempted to bring about significant change in their countries while trying to save some semblance of the current order. One of the most prominent examples in recent history is F. W. de Klerk's attempt to bring blacks into the political process as equals in South Africa.[4] Boris Yeltsin's struggle in late March and April 1993 to reform Russia draws unmistakable parallels to Gorbachev's tenure and specifically to what should and should not be done. This was illustrated by the words spoken by Gorbachev, now a private citizen, hours before Yeltsin claimed special powers to overcome parliamentary resistance: "My wish to the Russian President," he said, "is to take the initiative in his own hands."[5] In the above cases leadership played an essential role in the reform of states.[6] This leadership is of a particular type; understanding exactly what that type of leadership is helps us understand how best a leader should go about reform.

The central characteristic of reform leadership is that it offers change while preserving the present order or myth. Revolutionary leadership, on the other hand, destroys the present order. It is because significant change is often desired without the complete destruction of the present order that reform leadership is so important. In fact, change is often sought through reform for the explicit purpose of preserving the present order.

The Study of Leadership in Sovietology

Nevertheless, despite its importance, the concept of reform leadership has not often been explicitly studied and very little theory about it has been developed. This is partly because the concept has been studied in its constituent parts—*reform* and *leadership*. Notable exceptions are the literatures on private corporations and public bureaucracies (Breslauer, p. 313). A good example of this lack of scholarship is in the literature on the Soviet Union also known as Sovietology. Even though Russians and the students of that country have a profound bias towards the inclusion of leadership in their studies, Sovietology explicitly produced and utilized very little leadership theory in the analysis of Lenin, Stalin, Khrushchev, Brezhnev and Gorbachev. The Sovietologist who came closest to doing so in the 1950s was Nathan Leites (1951) in *The Operational Code of the Politburo*. The *pluralism* or *corporatism* debate during Brezhnev's regime discussed many leadership issues but did not develop theory. The scholarly debates concerning the role that Gorbachev played in the Soviet Union, though, did introduce leadership theory.

Sovietologists saw Gorbachev as a unique leader very different from his predecessors and this prompted some to seek the help of theory in explanation. Though significant parallels were made with Khrushchev, the "Gorbachev phenomenon" was treated separately from the former leaders. Kenneth Jowitt and Stephen Hanson analyzed Gorbachev and the Soviet "phenomenon" in general from a somewhat strict application of Max Weber's social theory and specifically from Jowitt's own highly insightful Weberian theories of Leninist development. Robert Tucker, who already possessed an interest in leadership and mass movements, conceptualized Gorbachev as a reform leader. George Breslauer, after an extensive review of the literature on private corporations and public bureaucracies, conceptualized Gorbachev as a transformational leader based on the work of James MacGregor Burns.

Tucker and Burns both describe a reform leader as having the characteristic of seeking change in order to preserve the current political order. Tucker states, "The reform leader, we have suggested, espouses the political community's sustaining myth, its professed ideal culture patterns, and defines the deviation of certain practices from those patterns as a wrong situation that can and should be corrected by changing the practices" (Tucker, p. 26). Burns quotes H. M. Kallen: "The reformer operates on parts where the revolutionist operates on wholes...(he) seeks modifications harmonious with the existing trends and consistent with prevailing principles and movements" (Burns, p. 170). Both clarify the concept of reform leadership by comparing it to revolutionary leadership. Burns writes, "The revolutionist seeks redirections, arrest or reversal of movements and mutation of principles. . . . It is this insistent exclusive particularism which distinguishes the reformer from the revolutionary as a psychological type. . . ." (Burns, p. 170). Tucker similarly states that, "Revolutionary leadership, on the other hand, sees and defines the collective situation as so irremediably wrong that the only possible solution is a fundamental reconstitution of society" (Tucker, p. 26).

Both Tucker and Burns correctly conceptualize leadership as a relationship between leaders and followers. Tucker explains that the need for leadership "arises when circumstances take on meaning for whole groups of people in such a way that diagnosis of their meaning is called for followed by action by the group or on its behalf to meet the situation as defined" (Tucker, p. 13). He specifies three phases of leadership activity; they are the diagnostic, policy-formulating, and policy-implementing phases:

1. **Diagnostic:** leaders are expected to diagnose group situations authoritatively, wisely and in good time.[7]
2. **Policy-formulating:** they must prescribe a policy, i.e., a course of group action or action on the group's behalf that will resolve the problem-situation.
3. **Policy-implementing:** leaders must gain the group's support, or predominant support, for the definition of the group situation that they have advanced and for the plan of action that they have prescribed.[8]

A political community's purposes and goals, which must be conceived by someone, are the standard by which divergences are compared and then determined to be political problem situations. Leaders and members of a community conceive the above affected by his or her group affiliations.

Tucker also describes the inseparable relationship between mass movements and leadership. Mass movements for change arise in response to non-constituted leadership when constituted or official leadership fails to diagnose problems and implement programs that the community or certain groups feel address problems relevant to them. These movements can be described as socio-political if they operate in and influence political life. If the movements become organized, then the former non-constituted leaders may become constituted leaders within the newly organized movements. And if the movements acquire state power, they become constituted leaders of states (Tucker, p. 15).

The concept of reform leadership for Tucker stems from the discussion of the concept of socio-political movements for change. Tucker splits socio-political movements into two categories: reform movements and revolutionary movements. But he argues that reform politics is much broader than reform movements. Why? Because he states that reform leaders are often heads of state or another type of constituted leader who may have furnished reforms without establishing a movement. There are some reform leaders, on the other hand, who do establish movements; for examples, he cites Franklin Roosevelt's New Deal administration and Gorbachev's administration in Moscow (Tucker, p. 20).

> **" THE EMPIRICAL EVIDENCE CLEARLY SUGGESTS THAT AUTHORITARIAN LEADERS FAIL AT MARKET REFORMS OR SIMPLY CHOOSE NOT TO IMPLEMENT THEM WITH VIGOR. "**

Reform leadership for James MacGregor Burns is a particular kind of transformational leadership in his elaborate theory. Transformational leadership occurs "when one or more persons engage with others in such a way that leaders and followers raise one another to higher levels of motivation and morality" (Burns, p. 20). This is contrasted to transactional leadership where one or more persons engage others for the purpose of an exchange of valued things; an example is a citizen's vote for a politician for the politician's promise of increased job opportunity. Transformational leadership and followers' purposes become fused and their power bases become linked in support of their common purpose. Ultimately, the relationship becomes moralistic because "it raises the level of human conduct of both leader and led, and thus it has a transforming effect on both." Burns cites Gandhi as the best modern example of this type of leadership because Gandhi "aroused and elevated the hopes and demands of millions of Indians and whose life and personality were enhanced in the process" (Burns, p. 20).

Reform leadership is contrasted with the other types of transformational leadership: intellectual, revolutionary, heroic and ideological. The reformer seeks modifications in line with the current trends and principles of society, while the revolutionary seeks to redirect or destroy the current trends and replace the current principles. Both seek to transform or change society. The intellectual leader emphasizes and clarifies the link between ends and means, where ends are values and purposes and means are political action and government re-organization for the purpose of change. Heroic leadership attracts belief not because of its stand on issues, capabilities, or experience, but for the personage of the leader. Ideological leadership promotes the goals and purposes of the movement or ideology in order to realize substantial social change. To reiterate, the emphasis of reform leadership is on change within the current order.

This study chooses Burns's typology to build on over Tucker's and simultaneously challenges the idea that reform leadership is a strict transformational process. Burns's typology deals with a wider range of leadership phenomena than Tucker's and does so for each in greater specifics. Second, recognizing that there is a major difference in the way that Tucker and Burns conceptualize a reform leader, I again prefer Burns's definition. However, Burns says a person morally uplifts both himself and his followers in transformational leadership, which includes reform leadership. A strong argument can be made for the need of a moral component as a part of transformational leadership as necessary to justify the substantial changes in the current order. Abraham Lincoln used morality as part of his reform leadership of the United States when he denounced slavery as wrong and, moreover, a distortion of what the American experiment in government was meant to be. Nevertheless, as one of the goals of this study is to understand whether reform is best practiced as a transactional or transformational form of leadership in today's world.

This study focuses on reformers in positions of executive leadership or power exclusively. Burns's typology of transactional leadership includes executive, legislative, group, party, and opinion forms of leadership. Comparing the effectiveness of leaders from twenty-three countries can be more soundly accomplished by narrowly focusing on executive leaders.

Transactional Reformers vs. Transformational Reformers
Should a reformer have transactional skills? Yes.

One of the key corollaries of this paper is that a reformer may be either transformation or transactional. Burns clearly places the reform leader in the transformational category while acknowledging that reform leaders may need the qualities of a transactional leader, specifically "a shrewd eye for opportunity, a good hand at bargaining, persuading, reciprocating" (Burns, p. 169). In fact, reform efforts of states in transition have a greater chance of success if bargaining between hard-line and more reform-minded elites takes place (O'Donnell and Schmitter, p. 39). Moreover, I would argue that the process of marketization requires shrewd bargaining skills.

Economic liberalization usually means either privatization of state industries, allowing prices of goods and services to find their fair market value, or both. The actual implementation of these policies, however, is highly problematic because of the negative effect it has on the ordinary citizen. Former Russian President Boris Yeltsin quickly learned in 1992-1993 that his economic programs not only caused pain among the general population but also gave his enemies issues on which he could be attacked. Yeltsin instituted shock-therapy reforms that included the liberalization of prices and the privatization of state property and industries whose elements and effects had not been fully thought through. Yeltsin's statements to the Russian people that the economy would get better were not satisfactory; no matter how hard he tried he could not uplift or transform the Russian people while they felt as if they were starving. Complex economic arrangements need complex bargaining solutions, and therefore require significant transactional skills. The question remains, however, how much transactional skill is necessary, or if transactional skill alone is sufficient.

Does a reformer need charisma? Maybe.
Reformers need charisma or other transformational skills if they have been brought in after a revolution has taken place and the order of things has not been preserved. Leaders in this situation must reconstitute a new set of myths, ideas, symbols and beliefs in order to bring society together once again. The old ideas and symbols have been discredited. It is at these points of conjuncture that Max Weber (1947) believes leaders have their greatest influence on the politics, society and culture of a country. However, is charisma the most important attribute of a reformer? If a state has not experienced a revolution where the unifying myths or order has been destroyed, then it may be the case that charisma is at the very least not sufficient to the success of the reform process.

Burns (p. 169) asks, "To what degree should reformers arouse popular hopes that may in turn be transformed into popular expectations and demands that run far beyond the leaders' specific aims?" This is a telling question: Boris Yeltsin aroused the hopes of the Russian people when he claimed that they would see their economic status improve after about a six-month period. When the economic status of the Russia people did not improve, he found himself in a struggle for power with the parliament. One might argue, therefore, that Yeltsin's attempt to use his charismatic, transformational skills backfired when his other skills could not effectively manage the economic reform program he had put into place.

Authoritarian vs. Democratic Reformers
Does A Strong Hand Lead to More Effective Reforms?

One persistent myth says that authoritarian leaders can more effectively institute economic reforms than democratic leaders. This myth argues that democratic leaders cannot effectively institute reforms if a citizenry object to the economic hardship usually associated with economic liberalization. In order for development to takeoff, capital must be concentrated and accumulated within a country. In order to maintain order while this takes place, the myth argues, political repression and central political control are needed:

> Demands by poor people for greater short-term consumption must be refused. Class disparities must be sharpened. Labor discipline must be enforced at extremely low wage levels. Foreign investors must be assured of political stability—above all, that radicals will not take power and that foreign assets will not be nationalized in a revolution. A democracy may be inherently incapable of accomplishing these difficult and painful tasks, according to this way of thinking (Goldstein, p. 595).

Authoritarian leaders, on the other hand, do not answer to the people; they derive their power and authority separate from the people even though they may work on their behalf. Examples of this type of leader have been drawn mostly from Asia—South Korea, Taiwan and China for example.

Nevertheless, for each example of authoritarian systems and leaders that have been successful there are also examples of authoritarian leaders who have failed. The vast majority of African dictators have failed famously to reform their economies. Moreover, many Latin American countries that replaced their military governments with civilian ones in the 1980s have seen their economic conditions improve (O'Donnell and Schmitter). In fact, convincing explanations for the economic success of countries in Asia have been presented that have taken the emphasis off the authoritarian nature of their leaders (Deyo).

Preliminary Conclusions
The empirical evidence clearly suggests that authoritarian leaders fail at market

reforms or simply choose not to implement them with vigor. I have conservatively only identified Presidents Aliev, Lukashenka, Nazarbayev, Akayev, Niyazov and Karimov as authoritarian leaders. Their respective countries can be classified as the following: three consolidated statist (anti-market economies) and three economies that are barely in transition towards a market economy. Moreover, the Freedom House Democracy and Economy Rankings for the same country are highly correlated with one another; all of the consolidated market economies have consolidated democracies, for example.

The empirical evidence so far does not clearly suggest whether or not transformational leaders do a worse job at leading market reforms. I have so far only identified Presidents Lukashenka, Havel, Shevardnadze, Walesa and Yeltsin as transformational reformers. Their above respective countries can be classified as the following: one consolidated statist (anti-market economy), two economies in transition towards a market economy, and two consolidated market economies. Although more empirical data will help to determine whether transformational or transactional leaders do a better job, detailed cases studies of the process by which leaders instituted reforms may shed the most light on the effects their leadership styles have had on their attempt to reform their states with success.

REFERENCES

Baylis, Thomas A. (1989). *Governing by Committee: Collegial Leadership in Advanced Societies.* Albany, NY: State University of New York Press.

Breslauer, George W. (1989). Evaluating Gorbachev as Leader. *Soviet Economy,* 5:4.

Burns, James MacGregor. (1978). *Leadership.* New York: Harper & Row.

Chirot, Daniel, ed. (1991). *The Crisis of Leninism and the Decline of the Left.* Seattle: University of Washington Press.

Colton, Timothy J., and Tucker, R. eds. (1995). *Patterns in Post-Soviet Leadership.* Boulder: Westview Press.

Dahl, Robert A. (1998). *On Democracy.* New Haven: Yale University Press.

Deyo, Frederic C., ed. (1987). *The Political Economy of the New Asian Industrialism.* Ithaca, NY: Cornell University Press.

Elgie, Robert. (1995). *Political Leadership in Liberal Democracies.* New York: St. Martin's Press.

Friedman, Thomas L. (2000). *The Lexus and the Olive Tree: Understanding Globalization.* New York: Anchor Books.

Gardner, John William. (1989). *On Leadership.* New York: Free Press.

Goldstein, Joshua S. (2001). *International Relations: Fourth Edition.* New York: Longman.

Hanson, Stephen. (1991). Gorbachev: The Last True Leninist Believer? *The Crisis of Leninism and the Decline of the Left.* Chirot, Daniel, ed.

Hough, Jerry F. (1997). *Democratization and Revolution in the USSR, 1985-1991.* Washington, DC: Brookings Institution Press.

Johnson, Paul. (1994). A World Without Leaders. *Commentary*, July.

Jones, Bryan D, ed. (1989). *Leadership and Politics: New Perspectives in Political Science.* Lawrence: University Press of Kansas.

Jowitt, Ken. (1990). Gorbachev: Bolshevik or Menshevik? *Developments in Soviet Politics.* White, Stephen, Pravda, A & Gitelman, Z., eds.

Kaplan, Robert D. (1997). Was Democracy Just a Moment? *The Atlantic Monthly*, Dec.

Kellerman, Barbara, ed. (1986). *Political Leadership: A Source Book.* Pittsburgh: University of Pittsburgh Press.

Leites, Nathan. (1951). *The Operational Code of the Politburo.* New York: McGraw-Hill.

O'Donnell, Guillermo, & Schmitter, P. (1986). *Transitions from Authoritarian Rule: Tentative Conclusions about Uncertain Democracies.* Baltimore: Johns Hopkins University Press.

Riker, William H. (1986). *The Art of Political Manipulation.* New Haven: Yale University Press.

Sheffer, Gabriel, ed. (1993). *Innovative Leaders in International Politics.* Albany, NY: State University of New York Press.

Tucker, Robert C. (1987). *Political Culture and Leadership in Soviet Russia.* New York: W. W. Norton & Company, Inc.

Walker, Mark Clarence. (1999). Vox Caesaris Vox Populi: Why and When Referendums are Called in the Post-Soviet States and Their Effects. (Ph.D. diss., University of California, Berkeley).

Weber, Max. (1947). *The Theory of Social and Economic Organization.* New York: Oxford University Press.

White, Stephen, Pravda, A. & Gitelman, Z. eds. (1990). *Developments in Soviet Politics.* Durham: Duke University Press.

Willner, Ann Ruth. (1984). *The Spellbinders: Charismatic Political Leadership.* New Haven: Yale University Press.

Wills, Gary. (1994). *Certain Trumpets: The Call of Leaders.* New York: Simon & Schuster.

Wren, J. Thomas, ed. (1995). *The Leader's Companion: Insights on Leadership Through the Ages.* New York: The Free Press.

Young, Oran R, (1991). Political Leadership and Regime Formation: On the Development of Institutions in International Society. *International Organization, 45:3,* Summer.

Zakaria, Fareed. (1997). The Rise of Illiberal Democracy. *Foreign Affairs,* Nov.-Dec.

MARK CLARENCE WALKER is an assistant professor of political science in the School of International Service at American University in Washington, D.C. Dr. Walker's research and teaching focuses on comparative politics, the Post-Soviet states, leadership, electoral politics and methodology. Professor Walker received his Ph.D. in political science from the University of California at Berkeley and his B.S. from the Massachusetts Institute of Technology.

---

[1] The term *power holder* is similar to James MacGregor Burns's term *power wielder*.

[2] The design of this study is similar to the design of my doctoral dissertation that was nominated by U. C. Berkeley's Department of Political Science for a Best Dissertation Award in the Ecological and Transformational Politics Section of the *American Political Science Association* (Walker 1999).

[3] Jerry Hough describes the breakup of the Soviet Union in 1991 as a "revolution" which was led by its constituent states, including Russia; in fact he describes the events in that time period as the "Second Russian Revolution" (Hough 1997). Likewise, the fall of Communism in Eastern Europe can also be described in revolutionary terms; nevertheless, each one of those states can also be said to have experienced a significant reform period following their "revolutions."

[4] Keller, Bill. (January 31, 1993). De Klerk's Gorbachev Problem: *The New York Times Magazine* , pp. 34-38, 42.

[5] Church, George J.(March 29, 1993). Yeltsin's Big Gamble: *Time,* vol. 141 no. 13, p. 21.

[6] The leadership of *states* is different from the leadership of *institutions.*

[7] Tucker is not more specific about what he deems as a "group" situation.

[8] These are his terms and definitions.

Leadership = Followership?

By Santiago Álvarez de Mon

OVER THE YEARS, THE TERM "LEADER" HAS ATTRACTED A BROAD spectrum of names that can easily include Lenin, Lincoln, Mussolini, Havel, Hitler, Gandhi, Castro, Jomeini, King, Mao Tse Tung, Milosevic or Mandela, just to name a few. From the viewpoint strictly of political science, there can be no question whatsoever that these people exercised a leadership function.

When I look over the list, I can only feel a degree of perplexity. Is the term "leader" so ambiguous that it lends its strength and color to so many diverse interpretations? A review of management literature leads one to conclude that a leader motivates us to do something we might be somewhat inclined to do. As James MacGregor Burns writes, "Leadership is a process of morality to the degree that leaders engage with followers on the basis of shared motives and values and goals…"[1] These are people who transmit positive currents of energy and mobilize forces hitherto dormant.

To awaken others, one must be awake. To motivate others, one must possess a wealth of drive and passion. How tough it is to lead a project or team without the enthusiasm and daring that only a leader can display! "Leaders whose pilot lights have died away will never be able to light up blazing bonfires in the members of their team," write the authors of *Why Teams Fail*.[2] The final product of a true leader is an indomitable will and the devotion to a cause that arouses commitment and obligation. What is the source of leaders' zeal and determination? Leaders possess an unwavering conviction that what they want is worth the effort, and they are absolutely persuaded that what they are doing is correct and appropriate. As K. Iamori writes, "Your passion is the source of success and accomplishment."[3] The paradigm of certainty guides leaders and encourages them to proceed and overcome the difficulties.

To accomplish this with style, leaders learn how to surround themselves with a loyal team of enthusiastic collaborators who can compensate for their leaders' weaknesses or shortcomings. In light of the variety and complexity of the goals at hand, the leader must rely on teamwork as an indispensable tool for success. "In my judgment," Peter Drucker writes, "the most effective leaders never say 'I', not because they have made a concerted effort to avoid using this word, but because they don't think in the first person singular: they think in terms of 'us', in terms of the team."[4]

In this journey through the characteristics and tasks of the leader, we inevitably come to the highest and most highly quoted summits. The essence of leadership, as many experts and apprentices so conclude, resides in the ability to communicate. *In Moments of Truth,* Jan Carlzon offers his own list of leadership competencies: "strategic, informer, listener, professor, and communicator."[5] There are people who, when they speak, cause others to snore. However, when leaders speak, others listen with dumbfounded fascination. This is the well of their incredible talent for seduction and human relations. The leader charms us, exerting a new and relentless influence on our thoughts and behavior. "Individuals who significantly influence the thoughts, behaviors, and/or feelings of others,"[6] notes Howard Gardner. Old habits, deep-rooted customs, enduring traditions find themselves undermined and questioned by the magic power of the leader. As in the movies, the handsome leading man enamours and captivates, enrapturing people otherwise skeptical. He displays a degree of personal charisma that adorns and distinguishes him. As Carly Fiorina, chairperson and CEO of Hewlitt-Packard, writes, "Charisma, force of personality, or interpersonal skills have often been stressed more than the brainpower required for leaders to think through problems and find new solutions."[7]

The leader possesses an unquestionable ability to transform. There is a before and an after. Human, political, and social reality, when subject to the leader's sorcery, undergoes change and transformation. Writes R. Semler, "I believe we have an organization that is able to transform itself continuously and organically."[8] This brings to mind the critical distinction between transforming and transactional leadership so clearly set out by Burns in his classic *Leadership.*[9] The word "change" is synonymous with transformation and is used often by prestigious authors when writing on leadership.[10] Inherent in the leader's craft is the management of change, the mobilization of underlying capacity to smother the resistance that men and women put up to the naturally dynamic nature of change.

This conflict that change inevitably brings presents another notion intimately connected to the idea of leadership. As Ronald Heifetz writes, "Music teaches that dissonance is an integral part of harmony. Without conflict and tension, music lacks dynamism and movement."[11] In describing the management style of Jim Burke at Johnson & Johnson and Andy Grove at Intel, Bennis defends creative tension: "Not only do they encourage dissent at the management level, they demand it and surround themselves with people smart enough to know the truth and independent enough to tell it."[12] Leaders are expert archeologists of human conflict.

Trial by conflict demands that leaders display tactical skills and an uncanny sense of precision. They not only know where they want to go, but they know what route they must take to get there. Here we witness the strategic capability inherent in leadership, without which many hopes and ambitions would be cut short. Fiorina sets the agenda with determination: "To change the company, you have to operate on the whole system – the strategy, the structure, the rewards, the culture."[13]

As we approach the end of our conceptual excursion, we enter into the deepest confines of the leader. What is the dream that the leader relentlessly pursues? What vision of the future? As Peter Senge answers, "Because it is tangible and immediate, a vision infuses the organization with shape and direction and helps people to set forward-driving goals."[14]

> ## " THE FINAL PRODUCT OF A TRUE LEADER IS AN INDOMITABLE WILL AND THE DEVOTION TO A CAUSE THAT AROUSES COMMITMENT AND OBLIGATION. "

This illuminating and futuristic vision governs and qualifies the extraordinary sense of mission of the leader. What is the ultimate rationalization of the project undertaken? What service is it that must be provided? "Call it mission or purpose," Senge writes, "it represents the fundamental reason for the existence of the organization. Why are we here?"[15] In essence, we are rendering a blueprint of the culture of the leader, a term meant to explain the wealth of principles, beliefs, ways, or patterns of behavior that have developed and taken root within the soul of an institution or a people. "The critical thing to understand about cultural dynamics is that leaders cannot arbitrarily change culture in the sense of eliminating dysfunctional elements, but they can evolve culture by building in its strengths while letting its weaknesses atrophy over time."[16]

Finally and obviously, leaders are leaders because they have followers. A lone, solitary leader is an insurmountable contradiction in terms. Peter Drucker addresses Max de Pree: "Max, a few minutes ago you stated that the primary task of a leader was to have followers. In fact, by its sole and only possible definition, a leader is someone who has followers."[17] Obviously, as a corollary to what has been said up to now, a leader achieves results that escape the ability of others. As Dave

Ulrich writes, "Our message to leaders may be put into the simple formula: Effective leadership = attributes x results."[18]

Perhaps the achievement of results explains the enormous power accumulated by so many leaders over the course of their time in management. No wonder James O'Toole devotes one of his sections to such a slippery subject in his *Leadership from A to Z*. "It's the real thing, the ability to influence others to accomplish something important and worthwhile."[19]

Perplexity and Ambiguity

After analyzing some of the keys of leadership, the question remains as to whether the subject has truly been probed in all its nature and scope. Can the natural ambiguity of the concept be penetrated with the help of expressions—vision, communication, change—that are themselves dual? Let me explain. Motivation. This is the rub, to get our people motivated toward achieving a chosen end. This sounds simple, but if we don't add something more, the idea of motivation laid out here could easily turn against us. What kind of motivation are we talking about? Purely extrinsic motivation, artificially advanced, or intrinsic and real motivation? Or rather should we talk of motivation as something that transcends our own person and self-interest and pushes us to mobilize our resources for others? "When I start a new business, there is one thing that I consider most important," writes Kazou Inamori. "I always ask myself: is my motive virtuous?"[20]

Using politics and history as a laboratory, and the dramatic biography of Adolph Hitler as a reference point, we see that motivation has a double edge: If only the Hitler youth had been less motivated and committed! Humanity would have been much better off had their idealized Fuhrer been a bit less impassioned and less determined toward his objective. As Heifetz writes, "By providing illusions of grandeur, internal scapegoats, and external enemies, Hitler misdiagnosed Germany's ills and brought his nation to disaster."[21]

Hitler possessed an unmistakable gift for communication capable of resonating in the minds and mobilizing the energies of people otherwise indifferent. Was this a strength or, paradoxically, a weakness? Wouldn't we be better off today if Hitler had been unable to hear or speak? Is the ability to communicate at the heart of leadership or is it an instrument that, when placed in questionable hands, can turn against each and every one of us? Shouldn't we place greater consideration on deeds and actions, the true and unequivocal instruments of dialogue, than on speeches or rallies where words can stifle sincerity?

Take the word "influence," for example. Doesn't it give off a detectable odor of moldable clay whose final shape depends on the potter's whim? There are healthy influences that restore hope in ourselves and in others. Likewise, there are influences that guide our thoughts and actions toward the vilest and most contemptible regions of mankind, where violence and sectarianism abide. Moving along this same line of thought, where do the processes for change and transformation, so closely tied to the leader's calling, take us in the end? What final judgment will time, the unyielding arbiter, ultimately hand down with its perspective and sense of proportion? What was Germany like in 1938? And in 1945? What was the final balance of the period of transformation so sadly embarked upon? Can we easily elude the judgment of history?

In the indispensable realm of results, an insufficient but inexorably necessary prerequisite, a multitude of additional questions emerge. What kind of results should we be talking about, purely quantitative results or qualitative outcomes as well? If we consider qualitative results, how should they be measured? What time frame should be considered? Are immediate results enough? The world is full of sprint artists. Or should we look for medium and long-term effectiveness? How

> ## " CAN THERE BE LEADERS WITHOUT FOLLOWERS, OR DOES THE MERE MENTION OF THE FORMER INCLUDE THE LATTER? "

should we evaluate, for instance, the management skills of a CEO? By sales, by market share, by stock market capitalization? What time frame should we keep in mind? Should we bring in additional variables such as jobs created, environmental impact, talent retention, organizational atmosphere, or educational level?

As for vision, was Adolph Hitler lacking in this faculty? Wasn't his dream one of a white Europe, pure and Aryan, an elite club reserved only for distinguished members? His was an exclusive, restrictive vision that made race and nationalism dominant values. He also possessed a deeply rooted sense of mission, working night and day in his quest. In this tireless struggle to convert his dream into reality, he tragically transformed it into a cause, an ultimate raison d'être, the final and definitive mission to which all his powers must unconditionally be subordinated. The final result was the defining of a new culture—a framework of institutions, symbols, and customs—that has come to be termed fascism. It was an oppressive and totalitarian culture that castrated the freedom and thought inherent in the human spirit, but regardless, it responds to the notion of culture as set down by custom and convention.

Finally, I want to conclude this part of my paper with a paradox formulated in the way of a question. Can there be leaders without followers, or does the mere mention of the former include the latter? Can certain leaders be questioned precisely because they have followers? By having followers, are they using arts that should morally deny them the status of leader? Inversely, isn't the loneliness of some demanding, questioning leaders precisely the irrefutable confirmation of the greatness and boundlessness of their design? Did Socrates have many followers when he began to pester the reigning Athenian orthodoxy with his obstinate obsession in pursuing uncomfortable inquiries? This man exercises a strong influence over me and today, many centuries after, I accord him the status of a moral and intellectual leader. But be that as it may, Socrates in his day suffered isolation and death. Galileo, Copernicus, Thomas More—the history of human civilization has afforded countless lone wolves that have written the most beautiful pages on the noble art of leadership.

Before I proceed in my proposition herein, allow me to inquire of those most inclined to confusing leadership with followers. What kind of "followership" are we talking about? Shall we measure out the same credit to free, independent, educated and responsible people who voluntarily and tentatively embrace the warmth of a common idea as we might measure out to a legion of serial clones that take refuge in the dim-witted comfort of the herd? Shouldn't all texts and treatises on leadership devote the same time and space to the flip-side of the coin, to the followers in need and in appreciation of their leader? To bring forward a personal conclusion, where does this tendency to follow someone come from? In following others, do we risk losing our selves irreversibly? What is more natural to the human being, to blindly follow the tracks left by a leader or, without abdicating or renouncing the healthy sociability of our nature, to find our own way and proceed accordingly? Where does the genesis of the concept of the leader ultimately lie? Isn't it the natural province of each human being to lead one's own life, to manage one's own career, and to live and write one's own unrepeatable biography?

Moral Dimension

What is the clarifying variable that enables one to know if the above ideas contribute to the progress of mankind? The answer lies in the notion of value, an elusive term for many scholars. A significant part of modern social sciences has moved toward a value-free approach, whereby scientific rigor requires the social sciences to throw off any attempt at studying what one ought to be. Rather, one must concentrate on the being, on what is observable and measurable, on empirical and numerical verification, giving up any possible study of values that might constitute a sort of spiritual escapism lacking in methodological commitment. Auguste Comte, founder of positivism, can be considered the precursor of this scientific rigor. Basically, Comte's most important ideal was to structure philosophy over purely scientific foundations. "The human spirit hereby renounces those absolute discussions that were only pertinent to philosophy in its infancy and hereby limits its efforts to mastering true observation, the sole possible foundation upon which true knowledge can be accessed and which is sensibly adapted to our true needs."[22]

As opposed to this scientific rigor that condemns social sciences to work with the same methodological instrumentation as exact sciences, the social scientist must be brave enough to advance a personal position, set out what philosophical values or ideas support it, explain the working method, accept reality, verify hypotheses, make the necessary modifications, and then be humble enough to allow for surprise, correct mistakes, and set off once again on the journey.

" **ONE OF THE GREATEST CHALLENGES A LEADER MUST FACE IS THE SEARCH FOR UNITY WITHIN DIVERSITY.** **"**

Why this epistemological parenthesis? Because I feel it is essential that values inherent to the human condition be present in any inquiry into leadership. Otherwise, the vacuum left could be filled in the most dangerous of ways. As R. Bellah writes, "Social science as public philosophy cannot be free of values. It accepts the canons of a disciplined, critical investigation, but it does not imagine that such an investigation can exist in a moral vacuum."[23] A contradiction arises if we opt for a value-free approach and then proceed to decry a leadership crisis, a lack of moral and political stature in those who govern.

Let our minds travel over the lands that make up our world. Human civilization, in the diverse ways it expresses its immense cultural commonwealth of languages, traditions, history, behavior patterns, social customs and religious beliefs, offers up an extensively broad range of lifestyles and ways and means. Fortunately, we are different in the color of our skin, in the language we speak, and in our beliefs and customs. If not, if we lived in a world of universal sameness, life would be a dull and colorless activity for sure. This multicultural diversity should be embraced as a remarkable opportunity to grow professionally and spiritually. Governing has much to do with respecting and addressing the differences rather than stifling them by means of an emasculating robot-like uniformity. This said, I believe that one of the greatest challenges a leader must face is the search for unity within diversity.

Carl Rogers states that "the most personal is the most universal."[24] When in the exchange of conceptual ideas and projects, one is capable of scratching through the surface and penetrating into the deepest realms of the social question, into the most private fiber of the human being, one stumbles onto the common universality of one's unfinished being. To probe beyond the epidermis and explore the common sediment among enduring men and women is probably the highest mission of a cosmopolitan and global leader. In this common substratum, the leader runs head-on into a series of timeless and universal values that must be promoted and practiced.

For Taylor, "human beings, whatever their nationality or passport, have intuitive feelings as to what constitutes right and wrong that transcends their will or whim."[25] Whether they act in accordance with these feelings is a separate question entirely. We find ourselves once again witnesses to the objective sovereignty of values, independent of their individual application. James Q. Wilson calls this common philosophical substratum the moral sense, inherently natural to the very substance of the human race. "By a moral sense, I mean an intuitive or directly felt belief about how one ought to act when one is free to act voluntarily."[26] Beyond cultural relativism, where all is debatable, where all depends ultimately on circumstances, on the interlocutor or on the moment, there exists a moral sense that naturally flows through all and which is universal. Karl Popper is another author who has approached the problem from various angles. "It is practically impossible to banish extra-scientific values from scientific activity. The situation is similar with regard to objectivity: we cannot strip the scientist from his propensity toward partisanship without stripping him of his humanity, nor can we eliminate or destroy his value judgments without destroying him as a human being and as a scientist."[27]

Now that I have addressed the axiological issues of the social inquiry that makes up my paper, I must necessarily show my cards and reassert myself on two great personal beliefs concerning the relationship between leadership and values. First leaders are either decent and noble, or they are not leaders in the philosophical sense of the word. If they are not guided by a passion and love for freedom and justice, then what other hidden power is guiding them? Second, leaders are not, nor do they wish to be, objective. How can they be objective and impartial in the wake of misery and injustice? How can they not furiously rebel against the slime and horror in which so many people on this planet live? In the two or three great issues that can be considered truly worthwhile, leaders are radicals in the literal sense of the term—they go straight to the root cause. They are passionate defenders of the weak, fierce enemies of the violent, belligerent campaigners for human dignity from the strength they get from the knowledge of what is morally right.

To construct the society that our new century is going to need, it is of capital importance that the best intellectuals rethink their attitude toward or relationship with concept of values—freedom, justice, friendship, solidarity—and reflect on the impact they can have on common society. Leader and values mutually overlap; to deny this duality and reciprocity is suicidal and irresponsible.

If what I want to write about is leadership, politics, and values, then I will appeal to a book whose title says it all in a nutshell: *Politics, the Art of the Impossible* by Vaclav Havel.[28] Let his words be your guide for now. "By politics with a spiritual dimension, I do not understand a politics that is merely a technological competition for power, limited to what can be practically achieved and seeking primarily to satisfy this or that particular interest. Nor do I mean a politics that is concerned merely with promoting a given ideological or political conception. And I certainly do not mean a politics based on the idea that the end justifies the means. I mean, rather, a politics deriving from the awareness that none of us—as individuals—can save the world as a whole, but that each of us must behave as though it were in our power to do so." To imbue politics with moral dignity, that is where Vàclav Havel, European citizen and statesman, exhibits his internal strength.

A Critical Reading of the Literature

In light of this philosophical approach, let us review some concepts set out above, the first of which is power. "Power teaches us what men are like," proclaims Sophocles. Is power an objective that in itself explains and justifies itself, bribing everything in its path, including the honesty and independence of the person who possesses it? Or is it perceived as a responsibility? Power can be nothing else than a powerful tool placed at the disposal of an edifying project or mission. As such, it demands free and humble personalities capable of staying free of its pitfalls and vanities.

Power, for what? Here is the existential doubt that refers us to the idea of service. Be it our family, a corporation, a hospital, a nation, all the people whom we respect and admire possess an exceptional helping of generosity and goodness capable of mobilizing others. An example is the leadership of the Girl Scouts of America assumed by Frances Hasselbein. The purpose of the organization: "to help each girl reach her own highest potential."[29]

This care in helping each person to realize his or her unfulfilled potential sheds a sublime interpretative light on the idea of mission. A good example of this can be found in the business leadership practiced by Konosuke Matsushita. What, for him, was the raison d'être of his company? To improve the human condition. "The mission of a manufacturer," he told employees in 1932, "is to overcome poverty, to relieve society as a whole from the misery of poverty and bring it wealth."

The humility that Matsushita appeals to allows for the development of a much more solid and robust shared leadership, as opposed to what usually arises around the supposedly irresistible personality of the leader.

> The best leader is one who is scarcely noticed, not one who is obeyed and acclaimed, nor one whom all despise. The good leader is one of few words, and when he has concluded his work and accomplished his purpose, the people will say: we did it. (Lao Tse) [30]

The use of the plural—we—restores normality and sobriety to a concept traditionally associated with magic and magnetism, with the charisma shown by special people. By extending the concept of leadership to a multitude of citizens and professionals, we provide a vision that gives expression to the fairest and most delicate viewpoint concerning the change process. As Gandhi said, "You must be the change that you want to see in the world." This moral and personalistic identity

" **A LEADER IS A POPULAR EDUCATOR WHO GIVES LESSONS IN THE CLASSROOM OF LIFE.** "

attributed to the process of leadership appeals as well to human communication. As Kim and Maugorgne write, "To hear the unheard is a necessary discipline to be a good ruler. For only when a ruler has learned to listen closely to the people's hearts, hearing their feelings uncommunicated, pains unexpressed, and complaints not spoken of, can he hope to inspire confidence in his people, understand when something is wrong, and meet the true needs of his citizens."[31] To hear the unheard… a mission impossible for so many leaders accustomed to vain euphoria and to the intoxication of the rally.

The concept of culture also reaches great heights through the power of solid and robust values. "Culture," D.S. Landes writes, "is the inner values and attitudes that guide a population."[32] And on the horizon, governing every step, every action, and every strategic move of the leader, is a broad and warm vision of the project undertaken. Every leader dreams, imagines and anticipates a brighter future, embraces an urgent calling, and feels a passion to achieve the goal. Martin Luther King was a dramatic and ultimately tragic case in point. "So I say to you, my friends, that even though we must face the difficulties of today and tomorrow, I still have a dream."[33] Was it reason, prudence, or science that enabled King to touch the sensitive fiber of the one million people who listened to him along the Capitol mall? We know very well that it wasn't. The positive currents of energy that penetrated the air that day were of a different sort.

The Challenge of Education

Stirring underneath everything I have been writing up to now is one of the central axioms of this paper. A leader is a popular educator who gives lessons in the classroom of life. Instead of provoking and tapping the worst in fellow humans, an easy, demagogic temptation for so many so-called leaders, a true leader becomes, as Gandhi wrote, "the poet who knows how to call forth with a powerful voice all that is good in the heart of man."[34] Assertions such as this explain why Heimo Rau, in *Great Soul,* affirms about Gandhi that "his method is based less on politics than on popular teaching."[35] Education in its deepest and most personalized dimension does not confine itself to the mere transmission from teacher to student of knowledge and know-how. It is something much more ambitious. It attempts to bring out the master that resides within every human being and to make it possible for ideas to thus burst forth. The best analogy that I know to express this idea can be found in Socrates's metaphor of the cave: education is "the movement from darkness to light," a long and dark journey, so much so that some people, blinded by the first lights of morning, want only to return to the old, familiar darkness.

The unwavering, almost obsessive commitment of leaders to the education of followers, favors the birth of another paradox. Leaders must work to become dispensable. To become changeable where today they are indispensable constitutes their supreme mission. They must be technically competent, skillful in the short sprints, morally consistent to aspire to the sobriety and simplicity of those who not only do not fear replacement, but who desire it for the good of the society they govern. To seek out, find, and prepare those leaders who are to manage the future, who are to prepare us for a better tomorrow, is the genuine acid-test of the leader, one who in the end will enable us all to draw sound conclusions on his or her true stature.

The society I believe in is built around well-prepared professionals, around citizens sensitive to the progress and destiny of their communities. It is led by people who, in spite of natural human limitations and shortcomings, refuse to live like marionettes. A mature society established on this triple foundation—professionals, citizens, persons—is or will be much more productive and prosperous than the other inactive, childlike society that enthrones and exalts its leaders. Societies that depend on vain, fickle egos that need to feed on the ignorance of the masses hide, at the same time, their future decadence and ruin. In more forceful terms, ignorance is the enemy, education is the scalpel, and the leader is the hand that skillfully plies it.

A Personal Journey

True leadership flows necessarily into the personal and inimitable. Such internal leadership is an extraordinarily important task in current society. Two authors, among many, Henry David Thoreau and Ralph Waldo Emerson made their names defending the freedom and dignity sacred to each individual. Thoreau, from the dear and creative solitude of his Walden Pond, places his bets unequivocally on the person as opposed to society: "The dull distinguish only races or nations, or at most, classes, but the wise man, individuals."[36] Emerson, in his classic essay "Self-Reliance," confirms that peace will only come when self-harmony prevails and when principles appear to rule human progress: "Nothing can bring you peace but yourself. Nothing can bring you peace but the triumph of principles."[37] From this distance in time and space, I hereby set out what for me is self-evident. Leadership is, before all else, a personal lesson; no one can study it for me. They can buy the books for me, set up a desk for me, hire a tutor for me, and give me vitamins to keep me alert. I appreciate this help, obviously, but in the end, the deep and profound dialogue must take place among three participants: life, the subject at hand, and the disciple, each in its own small and marvelous way. Leadership, therefore, has a lot to do with strength of character, with the courage to go back and retrace our steps along paths trodden by other solitary souls.

The words that Socrates addressed to the assembly that condemned him to death are perhaps the most eloquent testimony to the idea that to be yourself, to lead your life and career, to have your own ideas and projects in the simultaneously friendly and cruel ocean of human society, can be seen as an unforgivable boldness and provocation. Let us listen to him: "I have been condemned not for lack of words, but for boldness and nerve, for refusing to tell you what you so much like to hear, for not showing regret, weeping, or saying and doing many things unworthy of me, as I stated before and which you often hear from others."[38] Words old and new, bearers of the eternal duel between freedom and tyranny. The social, professional, economic and moral pressure can often become unbearable for souls less strong than Socrates. It is obvious that leadership requires courage and bravery.

This is the true motive of this paper: to encourage each person to be him— or herself instead of waiting for the arrival of a magical leader who, in the best of cases, will rock one to sleep. As the unfinished project which I am, a changing, constantly mutating reality, the personal inquiry into myself is not exempt from tension and internal grief, but these emotions are what toughen us. "Health is based to a certain degree on tension," V. Frankl writes, "the tension that exists between what has already been achieved and what remains to be achieved; or the empty gap between what one is and what one ought to be. This tension is inherent in human beings and, therefore, is indispensable to good mental health."[39]

In essence, we have a radical choice to make on a daily basis: either to become our worst enemy, torturing ourselves with extreme feelings of guilt and perfectionist scrupulousness, or to become our own best friend, the one we have always at hand. Once we accept ourselves as we are, an important change takes place that enables us to live with ourselves. The result is that I don't have to explain myself to others or demonstrate my talents or abilities; I simply accept myself as I am. The clarity and courage that comes from this acceptance constitutes the foundation of existence. "To grow does not mean leave oneself,"[40] Guardini writes. To leave oneself, to break with one's personal nature, is an imprudent turn in the road that many unconsciously take and come to ruin on.

"There exists only one truly serious philosophical problem: to judge whether life is worth living or not. The meaning of life is the most urgent question to be answered,"[41] exclaims Albert Camus. It is a question that only each person individually can hope to clear up. In seeking the answer, books, encyclopedias, advice and counsel from loved ones must quietly withdraw to allow the heart and mind to take over, where the best and most complete of all libraries can be built. Is this an exhausting proposition? Undeniably so, but the alternative, to resign from our condition, abdicate from our essence and to allow others, the pseudo-leaders, to govern us, is not only boring, but a dangerous and irresponsible project. Isn't it inherent in the human journey, at some point along the way, to stray off the trodden path left by others in order to break new paths? Isn't this turning point, with the genuine, mature, and free solitude that it entails, the beginning of a journey that ends in friendly company? Let us close, then, the childish and unrealistic myth of the leader, and let us create the true possibility of an authentic "utopia" based on the longing to build a social community founded on people who truly exercise their noble condition.

SANTIAGO ALVAREZ DE MON is a professor of organizational behavior at IESE Business School. He earned a law degree from Madrid University, a Master in Business Administration, from IESE Business School, and a Ph. D. in sociology and political science from the University of Salamanca. Author of three books: *The Human Corporation, Non-profit Sector: Challenges and Proposals for the 21st Century* and *The Myth of the Leader*. He is a visiting professor and consultant of leadership in different countries of America, Europe and Asia.

---

[1] Burns, James MacGregor. (1979). *Leadership*. New York: Harper Torchbooks.

[2] Robbins, H and Finley, M. (1999). *Why Teams Fail*. Barcelona: E. Granica.

[3] Inamori, Kazuo. (1995). *A Passion for Success. New York:* McGraw-Hill.

[4] Drucker, Peter. (1992). *Managing the Non-Profit Organization: Principles and Practices. New York*: Harper Business.

[5] Carlzon, J. (1989). *Moments of Truth.* USA: Harper Collins Publishers.

[6] Gardner, H. (1995). *Leadings Minds.* London: Harper Collins.

[7] Fiorina, Carly. (2000). *If You're a Leader, You've Got to Capture the Whole Person.* New York: Fortune, Oct. 16.

[8] Semler, R. (2000). *How We Went Digital Without Strategy.* Harvard Business Review, Sept. 1.

[9] Bennis, W. & Townsend, R. (1995). *Reinventing Leadership.* New York: William Morrow and Company, Incorporated.

[10] O'Toole, J. (1995). *Leading Change.* San Francisco: Jossey-Bass Publishers.

[11] Heifetz, R.A. (1996). *Leadership Without Easy Answers. Cambridge, MA:* The Belknap Press of Harvard University Press.

[12] Bennis, W. (1997). *Why Leaders Can't Lead.* USA: Jossey-Bass Publishers.

[13] Fiorina, Carly. (2000). *If You're a Leader, You've Got to Capture the Whole Person.* Fortune, Oct. 16.

[14] Senge, Peter. (1999). *The Fifth Discipline in Practice.* Editorial Granica.

[15] Senge, Peter. (1999). *The Fifth Discipline in Practice.* Editorial Granica.

[16] Schein, Edgar H. (January 1997). *Organizational Culture and Leadership- 2nd Edition. San Francisco, CA:* Jossey-Bass Business & Management Series.

[17] Drucker, Peter. (August 1992). *Managing the Non-Profit Organization: Principles and Practices. New York:* Harper Business.

[18] Ulrich, Dave. (1999). *Results-Based Leadership.* Harvard Business School Press.

[19] O'Toole, James. (1999). *Leadership from A to Z.* Jossey-Bass Publishers.

[20] Inamori, Kazuo. (1995). *A Passion for Success. NEW YORK:* McGraw-Hill.

[21] Heifetz, R.A. (1996). *Leadership Without Easy Answers.* The Belknap Press of Harvard University Press.

[22] Comte, A. (1993). *Discurso sobre el espíritu positivo.* Madrid: Alianza Editorial.

[23] Bellah, R. (1985). *Habits of the Heart.* Berkeley: University of California Press.

[24] Rogers, C. (1961). *On Becoming a Person.* Boston: Houghton Mifflin Company.

[25] Taylor, C. (1997). *The Ethics of Authenticity- 7th Edition.* USA: Harvard University Press.

[26] Wilson, James Q. (1993). *The Moral Sense.* New York: Simon & Schuster. Free Press Paperbacks.

[27] Popper, Karl. (1996). *In Search of a Better World. New York:* Routledge.

[28] Havel, V. (1997). *Politics, the Art of the Impossible.* New York: Alfred A Knopf.

[29] O'Toole, James. (1995). *Leading Change.* San Fransico: Jossey-Bass Publishers.

[30] Manz, C. & Henry P. Sims Jr. (1993). *Superleadership: Leading Others to Lead Themselves.* Barcelona: Ediciones Paidós. (cfr)

[31] Kim, W. Chan & Maugorgne, Renée A. (1992). *Parables of Leadership.* Harvard Business Review, July-Aug.

[32] Landes, D.S. (1998). *The Wealth and Poverty of Nations.* USA: W.W. Norton Company.

[33] Washington, James Melvin, ed. (1992). *I Have a Dream: Writings and Speeches that Changed the World.* San Francisco: Harper Collins Publishers.

[34] Gandhi, M. August. (1983). *Autobiography: The Story of My Experiments With Truth.* Dover Publishers.

[35] Heimo, R. (1994). *Great Soul.* Madrid: Ediciones Temas de Hoy. (cfr)

[36] Thoreau, H.D. (1975). *Selected Works.* Boston: Houghton Mifflin Company.

[37] Emerson, R.W. (1987). *The Essays of Ralph Waldo Emerson. Cambridge, MA*: Harvard University Press.

[38] Plato. *The Apology of Socrates and the Crito. Santa Barbara, CA:* Bandanna Books.

[39] Frankl, V. (January 1998). *Man's Search for Meaning. New York:* Washington Square Press.

[40] Guardini, R. (1983). *La aceptación de sí mismo y las edades de la vida.* Madrid: Ediciones Cristiandad.

[41] Camus, A. (1996). *Obras completas.* Alianza Editorial.